The Severn Valley

THE SEVERN VALLEY RAILWAY

John Marshall

DAVID ST JOHN THOMAS PUBLISHER

British Library Cataloguing in Publication Date
Marshall, John, *1922 May 1–*
The Severn valley railway.
1. England. Severn valley region Railway
services. 1980
I. Title
385'.09424

ISBN 0-946537-45-3

First published 1989 by
David St John Thomas Publisher
Reprinted 1991

Printed by Redwood Press Ltd, Melksham
for David St John Thomas Publisher
PO Box 4, Nairn, Scotland IV12 4HU

Contents

Introduction

The present Severn Valley Railway, running from Kidderminster in Worcestershire to Bridgnorth in Shropshire, has achieved the distinction of being one of the finest privately restored railways in the world. Other lines may have a longer route, traverse more spectacular scenery, operate older locomotives or trains, possess the unique charm of a narrow gauge, but few have met with such outstanding success as the SVR. In 1986, for example, it operated on 168 days, less than half the year, yet it carried 185,053 passengers, an average of over 1,100 on each operating day. On the last day of 1988 the total passengers for the year reached over 200,000 for the first time.

We must be careful with the word 'preserved'. Every railway is preserved as long as it operates, whether it be Paddington to Reading, or the West Highland. The significance of a line like the SVR is that it preserves something which would otherwise have been totally lost: steam-hauled trains on a quiet country branch line, with its attractive little stations and signal boxes, sharp curves and abrupt gradients, that were once so much a part of the British landscape, but which has now almost vanished.

For most of its length the railway runs through quiet river scenery, woods and fields, serving the old-world towns of Bewdley and Bridgnorth. The history of the railway forms only a minute part of the entire history of the Severn valley below Shrewsbury, and it is interesting to look briefly at this before turning to the railway.

CHAPTER 1

The Valley

The Severn valley, from Ironbridge southwards to the Bristol Channel, is geologically recent. Until the last ice age, about 25,000 years ago, the upper Severn flowed into a lake of irregular shape, about 35 miles east to west and about 25 miles north to south, surrounding what is now Shrewsbury about 270ft above present sea level. This lake drained into the Trent basin near where is now Gnosall, Staffordshire. During the ice age no water flowed because it was all solid ice. When this melted the old outlet became blocked, probably by ice; the level of the lake rose to about 300ft, and the water began to spill over the rock barrier where Ironbridge is. Once the lake began to drain here the water rapidly cut what we now call Ironbridge Gorge and formed the present course of the lower Severn.[1] The river thus divides itself into three portions: the gorge-like upper Severn from its source down to below Welshpool; the central portion where it meanders across the ancient lake bed around Shrewsbury; and the more recent lower portion down the glacial spillway which maintains a fairly direct course from Buildwas to its outlet below Gloucester.

The name of the river has changed little over the centuries. Its Celtic name, *Sabrina*, is recorded as early as 115-117, and in its English forms the name *Sabrena* dates from 706, and *Saeferne* from 757-75. Other recorded changes are: *Seferne* in 851, *Severne* in 986, and *Saverne* in 1140. In its modern form the name *Severne* is recorded in 1439 and *Severn* in 1540. Throughout this period the pronunciation was probably roughly the same.[2]

Notes to this chapter will be found on p213.

Stone-age remains discovered around Gloucester, carried down the river when the valley was formed, prove that human settlements along its banks date from prehistoric times. The earliest historical settlers were the Romans who established towns at Wroxeter, 10 miles below Shrewsbury, and at Worcester and Gloucester. Shrewsbury developed before 900 on a glacial ridge of sand and gravel forming an easily defended site within a meander. A castle was built at a point where the bends in the river are only 300 yards apart and just below this, partly on a bridge across the river, stands the present Shrewsbury station.

Just above the Ironbridge Gorge, at Buildwas, the abbots of the Savignac Order founded Buildwas Abbey in 1135 as an offshoot of Furness Abbey. It was occupied by the Cistercians until the Dissolution. Lower down the river, at what is now Bridgnorth, a castle was built in 912, instituted by Ethelfleda, 'The Lady of the Mercians', daughter of Alfred the Great. This is believed to have been the mound known as 'Pan Pudding' or 'Pam Pudding' Hill, close to Bridgnorth station, but this is not certain, although there is no doubt that this was an early fortified site. The later Bridgnorth castle, at the more obviously defendable site on the sandstone bluff above the river, was established about 1101 by Robert de Belleme, son of Roger de Montgomery, where he transferred the church and borough from Quatford two miles down the river. The first bridge was built at Bridgnorth about the same time. In April 1646 Cromwell's forces used Pan Pudding Hill as a site from which they bombarded Bridgnorth castle for three weeks. When the royalists in the castle surrendered, the castle was blown up by gunpowder. Hence the crazy angle at which part of it is tilted.

About 12 miles below here, where the river could be forded at low water - and it should be noted that before the construction of weirs in the lower reaches it was tidal this far inland - the Saxons formed a settlement on the left bank and called it Gurbehale, which name finally became Wribbenhall. Across the ford the town of Bewdley grew on the west bank.

The name derived from the Norman Beaulieu, or beautiful place. This had become Beaudley when its first charter was granted in 1472. Fifteen miles farther down, Worcester became established at a point where the river could be fairly easily forded; here human settlement is traced back to 2000 BC. Gloucester, at the lowest place at which the river could be crossed, became an important Roman station.

Navigation on the Severn antedates even the earliest settlements, and 500 years ago the river was carrying more traffic for a greater distance than any other river in Britain. By the time the first bridge was built at Bewdley in 1336 the town had become an important inland port. The Severn was never an easy river to navigate. At all times the current is strong; in flood it sweeps down at frightening speed, and at other times shallow places form obstructions where the river dashes over rocks.

A race of hefty men known as 'bow hauliers' developed to drag the boats up stream. Improvements were made in the form of paths along the banks under Acts of 1503 and 1531-32 which provided for their maintenance, and by these means the shallow draft 'Severn trows' could be hauled up to Bewdley. Above here smaller vessels could reach Coalbrookdale and Shrewsbury and even smaller ones went up as far as Welshpool.

A writer in *Gentleman's Magazine* in 1756 reported that above Bridgnorth there were a hundred owners of barges and trows with a total of 172 vessels. Between Bridgnorth and Gloucester there were 210 owners with 376 vessels.[3] The cost of freight shipped from Shrewsbury to Bristol was 10s per ton and from Bristol to Shrewsbury 15s.

South of Bridgnorth the river cuts through the Wyre Forest coalfield. Mining in this area dates back to early mediaeval times. Coal from the primitive workings was carried down to the Severn on pack horses. Around Coalbrookdale and the Ironbridge Gorge coal was mined before the reign of Queen Elizabeth 1. James Clifford, a coal owner of Broseley, made a practice of tipping spoil from his pit at Tuckies into the Severn. By 1575 it was forming an obstruction to navigation and he was ordered by the Severn Commissioners to remove it at his own expense. A wooden railway, one of the earliest in the country, linked pits at Calcutts near Broseley to the Severn in 1605.[4] Bewdley became an important distribution centre for coal and the wharf above the bridge was known as 'Coles Quay' until quite recently when it was changed to 'Severnside North'.

Another important industry in the valley was iron smelting. At Coalbrookdale, ironworks were established in the 16th century and had been at work for over a century and a half by the time the Coalbrookdale Company was formed in 1709. Coalbrookdale has been described as the cradle of the Industrial Revolution. From the 'blowing in' of the first Horsehay furnace by Abraham Darby II in 1755 the iron industry expanded rapidly and this made possible the construction of the first iron bridge, over the Severn, in 1779, which gave its name to the town of Ironbridge which grew on the east bank. The first cast-iron wagonway rails were made at Coalbrookdale in 1767. The world's first steam locomotive was built here by Richard Trevithick in 1803 for the 3ft gauge plateway, but there is no evidence that it actually ran.

The decline of Bewdley as a port dates from the completion of the Staffordshire & Worcestershire Canal in 1772. This followed the valley of the Stour down to the Severn where extensive basins gave rise to the town of Stourport. In an attempt to arrest Bewdley's decline an Act was obtained in 1772, the year the canal opened, to form a towing path for horses from Bewdley up to Coalbrookdale with tolls of 7s per horse up to Bridgnorth and 5s from there to Coalbrookdale. A second Staffordshire & Worcestershire Canal Act in 1790 enabled the canal company to improve the Severn navigation from Stourport down to Worcester. Another towpath Act in 1809 gave powers to build a towpath from Coalbrookdale up to Shrewsbury.

A railway to connect Bewdley with the canal at Kidderminster was projected in September 1801 and a plan and section were prepared to a scale of 4 chains to 1 inch. The drawings are not signed and there is no indication of who was the engineer. The plan showed the railway starting beside the Severn at Wribbenhall, running along the north side of the Kidderminster road for a mile then turning to the north, through private land to a summit of 193ft at High Habberley, from where it descended to the canal opposite St Mary's and All Saints church at Kidderminster.[5] No Act was obtained and no work was carried out. The railway could have done little to arrest Bewdley's decline as a port.

The Shropshire Canal Company, incorporated in 1788 to construct a canal to link mines and ironworks around Oakengates with the Severn, used inclined planes to connect with the Wombridge and Donnington Wood canals and terminated 333ft above the Severn at the head of the Hay inclined plane. This was completed with an engine in 1792. At its foot it entered the Coalport Canal which ran parallel to the Severn, and a little above it, to terminate at a series of wharfs by which the coal could be transferred from the tub boats to the river vessels. A village grew up here with the name Coalport. A timber bridge over the Severn, built in 1780, was replaced by the iron Coalport bridge in 1799, of a design showing a great advance in the use of iron since the iron bridge of twenty years earlier. At its peak coal traffic shipped from Coalport reached 100,000 tons per year and as many as 70-80 vessels could be seen loading at the quays.

Between 1778 and 1790 ironworks were established at Eardington and Hampton Loade. (Loade comes from the Saxon 'lode' meaning ford.) Iron foundries were developed also at Bridgnorth; here John Hazeldine was joined by William Foster in 1807 and together, in 1808, they built Richard Trevithick's fourth and last locomotive *Catch me who can* which Trevithick demonstrated in London, an event commemorated on a plaque on the clock tower at the east end of the Bridgnorth bridge.

The iron industry on the Severn reached its peak in the 1790s and then began to decline as other activities, principally clay industries producing bricks, tiles and pottery, came to the fore.

The Hampton Loade ironworks closed in 1866 and the upper and lower forges at Eardington, which used pig iron brought down the Severn from Coalbrookdale, closed in 1889.[6]

The last important canal to reach the Severn, the Worcester & Birmingham, was opened throughout on 4 December 1815. The Lowesmoor basin, off this canal in Worcester, was the intended southern terminus of the earliest railway scheme to link Shrewsbury and Worcester, projected through the Severn valley in 1846. The Severn Navigation Act of 1842 gave powers to construct weirs and locks between Gloucester and Worcester (at Upton) and between Worcester and Stourport. These were carried out under William Cubitt with Edward Leader Williams as sub-engineer, and together with the Gloucester & Berkeley Canal, completed in 1827, they opened up a reliable navigation from Stourport to the sea.[7]

CHAPTER 2

Preliminary Surveys

The projectors of Britain's earliest railways were concerned about linking the major towns to the exclusion of places in between. The Grand Junction Railway, opened in 1837, missed Wolverhampton; the Birmingham & Gloucester, opened in 1840, missed Bromsgrove, Droitwich, Worcester, and almost missed Cheltenham and even Gloucester. Neither were they eager to co-operate with their neighbours. The poor facilities for through traffic between the GJR and the London & Birmingham at Birmingham, and the lack of any railway accommodation at Wolverhampton caused Black Country industrialists, in 1845, to project the Oxford, Worcester & Wolverhampton Railway (OWW) from the GWR north of Oxford to a junction with the GJR north of Wolverhampton, by-passing Birmingham altogether. The first section to be completed, from Worcester to a junction with the Midland (former Birmingham & Gloucester), at Abbots Wood Junction near Norton, was opened on 5 October 1850. This at last placed Worcester on the railway map, and with its opening to Droitwich and the Midland again at Stoke Works Junction, on 18 February 1852, Worcester was connected directly to Birmingham. By the end of 1852 the OWW was opened from Droitwich to Dudley via Hartlebury, Kidderminster, and Stourbridge

Shrewsbury became the focal point of a number of lines all authorised within a few weeks in 1846. The Shrewsbury

Notes to this chapter are on p213.

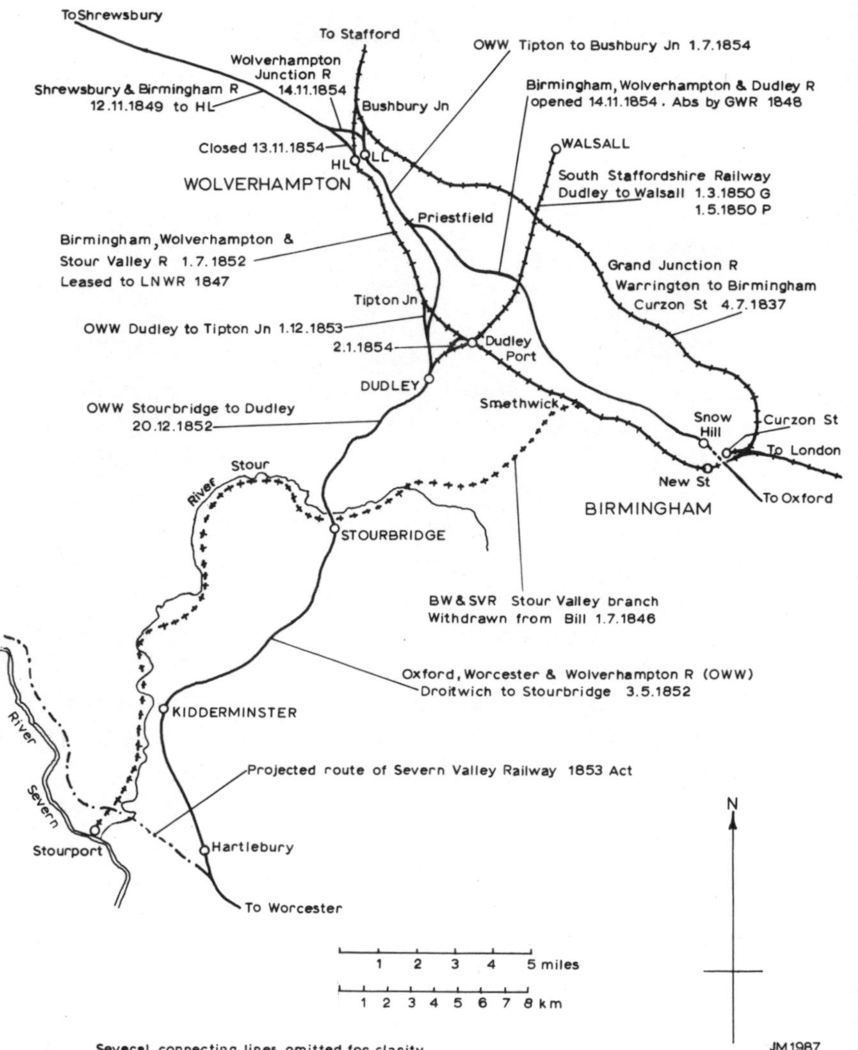
WEST MIDLANDS RAILWAYS 1854
To Shrewsbury
To Stafford
Wolverhampton Junction R 14.11.1854
Shrewsbury & Birmingham R 12.11.1849 to HL
OWW Tipton to Bushbury Jn 1.7.1854
Birmingham, Wolverhampton & Dudley R opened 14.11.1854. Abs by GWR 1848
Bushbury Jn
Closed 13.11.1854
HL
LL
WOLVERHAMPTON
WALSALL
South Staffordshire Railway Dudley to Walsall 1.3.1850 G 1.5.1850 P
Priestfield
Birmingham, Wolverhampton & Stour Valley R 1.7.1852 Leased to LNWR 1847
Grand Junction R Warrington to Birmingham Curzon St 4.7.1837
Tipton Jn
OWW Dudley to Tipton Jn 1.12.1853
2.1.1854
Dudley Port
DUDLEY
Smethwick
OWW Stourbridge to Dudley 20.12.1852
Snow Hill
Curzon St
To London
New St
To Oxford
BIRMINGHAM
River Stour
STOURBRIDGE
BW & SVR Stour Valley branch Withdrawn from Bill 1.7.1846
Oxford, Worcester & Wolverhampton R (OWW) Droitwich to Stourbridge 3.5.1852
KIDDERMINSTER
River Severn
Projected route of Severn Valley Railway 1853 Act
Stourport
Hartlebury
To Worcester
N
1 2 3 4 5 miles
1 2 3 4 5 6 7 8 km
Several connecting lines omitted for clarity
JM 1987

& Chester was to take over the Shrewsbury, Oswestry & Chester whose Act was passed the previous year. No less than six railways affecting Shrewsbury were authorised by Acts passed on 3 August 1846; the Shrewsbury & Hereford; the Shropshire Union Railways & Canal; the Shrewsbury & Birmingham; Wolverhampton & Dudley; and the Birmingham, Wolverhampton & Stour Valley; the last so named because it included a branch through the Stour Valley to Stourport, which was withdrawn from the bill. (See map p16) The Railway Mania was then at its height; in 1846, 272 railway bills received the Royal Assent, the greatest number in any year, and many more failed. The Shrewsbury, Wolverhampton & South Staffordshire Junction, being identical to the Shrewsbury & Birmingham between Shrewsbury and Wolverhampton, was not proceeded with.

Of these the first to be completed was the Shrewsbury & Chester, opened throughout on 16 October 1848. The Shropshire Union planned several lines including, as will be mentioned later, one down the Severn valley, but all that was completed was the line from Shrewsbury to Stafford, leased to the LNWR in 1847 and opened on 1 June 1849. The section from Shrewsbury to Wellington was built jointly with the Shrewsbury & Birmingham which, on the same day, was opened to Oakengates. The section from Oakengates to Wolverhampton was opened on 12 November 1849. At Wolverhampton it was connected with the Birmingham, Wolverhampton & Stour Valley. This, with the Shropshire Union, was leased in 1847 to the LNWR which built it and opened it on 1 July 1852.

The complex history of the Shrewsbury & Birmingham can concern us only briefly. Disputes at Wolverhampton resulted in its alliance with the GWR, which had absorbed the Birmingham, Wolverhampton & Dudley in 1848. The Shrewsbury trains, after running via the LNWR to Birmingham New Street from 4 February 1854, were rerouted on 14 November via the new Wolverhampton Junction line into the Low Level station at Wolverhampton and to Birmingham Snow Hill. Together with the Shrewsbury & Chester, the S&B amalgamated with the GWR on 1 September 1854.

Meanwhile the OWW, which we had left at Dudley, was extended to a temporary junction with the LNWR 'Stour Valley' line at Tipton, so enabling the trains to reach Wolverhampton High Level on 1 December 1853. The line was completed to Wolverhampton Cannock Road on 1 July 1854 and was joined at Priestfield by the GWR line from Birmingham Snow Hill on 14 November, and together they were connected with the S&B at Wolverhampton Low Level. Southwards the OWW was opened to Wolvercote Junction north of Oxford on 4 June 1853.

Throughout this period attention was being focussed on the Severn Valley from Shrewsbury down to Worcester as affording a good railway route. The first positive step was taken by the Shropshire Union Railways & Canal Co which employed no less a person than Robert Stephenson to direct a survey through the valley and to prepare plans and sections for a bill. Assisted by Frederick Swanwick (1810-85) who, at that time like Stephenson, was engaged on so many other railway projects that he could not have spent much time in the valley, he produced the plan and section during 1846. A bill was drawn up by Parker, Hayes, Barnwell & Twisden of 1 Lincoln's Inn Fields, London, and was advertised in the local press in Shrewsbury and Worcester during November. The bill was deposited on 30 November but the SU, with too many schemes in hand at once, was unable to proceed with the Severn Valley project. However, since its route was closely followed later it is worth examining.

From a west-facing junction with the authorised line of the Shrewsbury & Birmingham Railway near Shrewsbury race course just north of the Abbey, the line was to follow a south-easterly course past Berrington, Cound, Cressage, beside Buildwas Abbey and through the Ironbridge Gorge. Closely following the right bank of the river, it entered the estate of Thomas Charlton Whitmore of Apley Park. Whitmore was

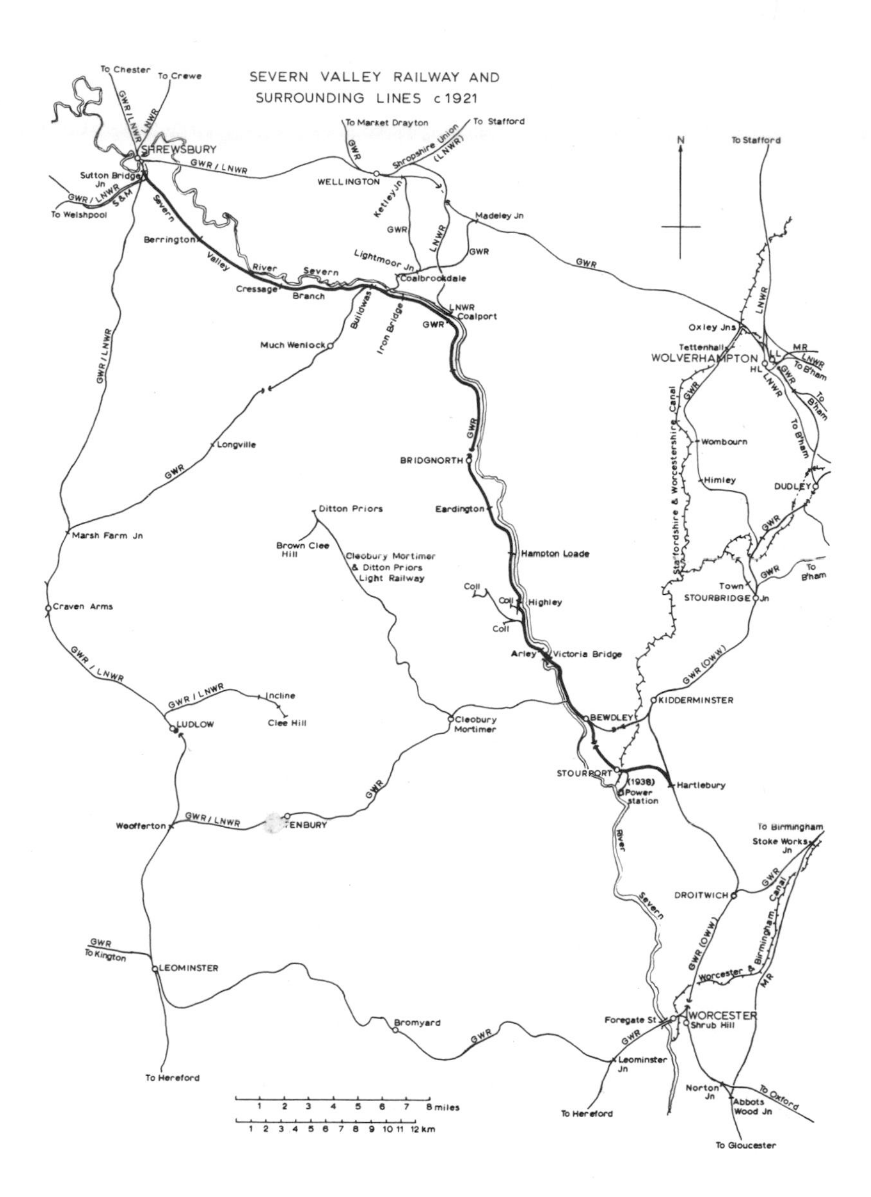
SEVERN VALLEY RAILWAY AND
SURROUNDING LINES c 1921
To Chester
To Crewe
GWR/LNWR
LNWR
SHREWSBURY
GWR / LNWR
Sutton Bridge Jn
GWR / LNWR
S&M
To Welshpool
Severn
Berrington
Valley
River
Severn
Cressage
Branch
To Market Drayton
To Stafford
GWR
Shropshire Union (LNWR)
WELLINGTON
Ketley Jn
GWR
LNWR
Madeley Jn
GWR
Lightmoor Jn
Coalbrookdale
Buildwas
Iron Bridge
LNWR
Coalport
GWR
Much Wenlock
GWR
GWR/LNWR
Longville
GWR
BRIDGNORTH
Eardington
Ditton Priors
Brown Clee Hill
Cleobury Mortimer & Ditton Priors Light Railway
Hampton Loade
Coll
Coll
Highley
Coll
Arley
Victoria Bridge
Marsh Farm Jn
Craven Arms
GWR / LNWR
GWR / LNWR
Incline
Clee Hill
LUDLOW
Cleobury Mortimer
GWR
Woofferton
GWR / LNWR
TENBURY
BEWDLEY
STOURPORT
(1938)
Power station
Hartlebury
KIDDERMINSTER
GWR (OWW)
River
Severn
N
To Stafford
LNWR
Oxley Jns
Tettenhall
WOLVERHAMPTON
LL
HL
MR
LNWR
To B'ham
GWR
LNWR
To B'ham
To B'ham
GWR
Wombourn
Staffordshire & Worcestershire Canal
Himley
DUDLEY
GWR
GWR
To B'ham
Town
STOURBRIDGE Jn
To Birmingham
Stoke Works Jn
DROITWICH
GWR
Canal
Worcester & Birmingham
GWR (OWW)
MR
WORCESTER
Shrub Hill
Foregate St
GWR
Leominster Jn
To Hereford
Norton Jn
Abbots Wood Jn
To Oxford
To Gloucester
GWR
To Kington
LEOMINSTER
Bromyard
GWR
To Hereford
1 2 3 4 5 6 7 8 miles
1 2 3 4 5 6 7 8 9 10 11 12 km

to prove a thorn in the flesh for the SVR. He was born at Apley on 6 January 1807 into a family tracing its ancestry back to the reign of Henry III, and from 1832 to 1852 he was Conservative MP for Bridgnorth. In 1863 he was High Sheriff of Shropshire. He insisted that the railway should be out of sight so as not to spoil his outlook from the house. So, at 18 miles 2.75 furlongs, the line was to enter a tunnel 440yd long and a short distance beyond this another tunnel of 143yd. At Bridgnorth the line was to pass under the town in a tunnel of 594yd. Opposite Arley, at 30 miles 3f, was a tunnel of 391yd, south of the present station, beyond which the line was to cross the Severn. Through Wribbenhall, opposite Bewdley, the line continued through a tunnel 209yd long under Mount Pleasant and crossed the Bewdley - Stourport road. From here it closely followed the river and terminated at the Lowesmoor canal basin in Worcester, almost 48 miles from end to end. A branch in Worcester, $^1/_2$ mile short of the terminus, crossed the Worcester & Birmingham canal and joined the authorised line of the OWW just north of where Shrub Hill station would be built.

There were to be three other branches: first from a south-facing junction in the parish of Benthall, across the Severn into Coalbrookdale, through a 274yd tunnel, past the ironworks, through another tunnel of 436yd, to a junction with the proposed Coalbrookdale branch of the Shrewsbury & Birmingham, 1 mile 1.72f; second, from another south-facing junction below Broseley, across the Severn, then via Madeley and Stirchley (close to the route later followed by the LNWR Coalport branch) to another junction with the Coalbrookdale branch of the S&B, 2 miles 3.75f; third, a branch from a south-facing junction at Lower Mitton, Stourport, to Kidderminster, 3 miles 2.65f.

Although the SU failed to go further with the project it was not allowed to die, but was taken up by interested parties who employed Robert Nicholson to carry out another survey in 1849. Nicholson, born in Northumberland on 31 August 1808, trained as a surveyor and worked on several

HERAPATH'S JOURNAL. JUNE 26, 1852.

Severn Valley Railway.

SHREWSBURY to WORCESTER.

Capital, £350,000, in 14,000 shares of £25 each.

Deposit, £2 2s.

Under the sanction of the following Proprietors of estates, and other parties locally interested upon the line:—

His Grace the Duke of Cleveland,
The Right Rev. the Lord Bishop of Worcester,
The Right Hon. Lord Forester,
Sir John Dean Paul, Bart,
Sir Thomas E. Winnington, Bart.,
Thomas Charlton Whitmore, Esq., M.P.,
William Wolryche Whitmore, Esq.,
William Lacon Childe, Esq.,
The Mayor and Corporation of Bridgnorth,
The Coalbrookedale Company,
The Lilleshall Company,
&c., &c., &c.

A COMPANY is in the course of formation to construct a railway directly connecting Shrewsbury and Worcester, and to afford to the important districts along this portion of the Valley of the Severn the benefits of railway communication.

The proposed line will leave the Madeley Branch of the Shrewsbury and Birmingham Railway near to Madeley, and proceed direct to Bridgnorth, and thence follow the Valley of the Severn by Bewdley and Stourport, near which latter place it will fall into the Oxford, Worcester, and Wolverhampton Railway, thus affording railway accommodation to the towns and districts of Coalbrookdale, Ironbridge, Coalport, Madeley, Broseley, Much Wenlock, Bridgnorth, Bewdley, Kidderminster, and Stourport.

The line will also, in connection with other railways, establish the shortest route between Worcester and the whole of the South West of England and Wales on the one hand, and Chester, Birkenhead, Holyhead, and the North of Ireland and Wales on the other.

As regards the local requirements of the line, the enumeration of the towns and districts that will be served by it, and which are at present without railway accommodation, is considered sufficient. It should, however, be stated that the difficulty of navigating the Severn above Stourport has long called for some better means of transit in those parts.

The proposed line is about twenty six miles in length, and the country through which it will pass well suited for the formation of a railway; the landowners have been consulted and are favourable to the project.

It is obvious that the construction of this line will be beneficial to the existing railways it is intended to join; the line is, in fact, the natural extension of the Oxford, Worcester, and Wolverhampton Railway, which Company it is expected will give its support to the undertaking.

A preliminary survey of the line has been made, and a detailed prospectus will be shortly issued; communications in the meantime may be addressed to Messrs. H. and W. Toogood, 22, Parliament-street, London.

June, 1852. (3943)

Tyneside railway projects. He was a close associate of Robert Stephenson. By now the OWW was planned, so to shorten his line Nicholson began it from a junction with the OWW south of Hartlebury station. It passed south of Hartlebury village and Castle and round the north of Stourport, and from there closely followed Robert Stephenson's line as far as near Quatford, south of Bridgnorth. Here it crossed the Severn and passed through Bridgnorth Lower Town, east of the bridge. From this point it passed to the east of Apley Park to join the Madeley branch of the S&B near Madeley. By this means it avoided the opposition of T.C. Whitmore of Apley. On 26 June 1852 the advertisement on page 21 appeared in *Herapath's Railway Journal.*

It will be noted that T.C. Whitmore had given his approval. The first meeting of the SVR board at the office of W. Toogood, Westminster, was on 25 August 1852 when Jonathan Thorp, William Reed, M. Grazebrook and Major Tyndale resolved to form a company to be called the Severn Valley Railway Company.[1] Seven directors were appointed and Robert Nicholson was the engineer. At the following meeting on 6 September it was decided to hold public meetings to encourage local support. These were arranged at Ironbridge, Bewdley and Bridgnorth on 7, 8 and 9 October. At all of these meetings it was the general wish that the line should be extended to Shrewsbury, and so on 13 October the board decided to do this and to provide a double line with a branch 'to the mineral districts'. The somewhat strange proposal was made to arrange for Samuel Morton Peto, the famous railway contractor, to carry out the works in return for his support for the project. The usual procedure was to put the works out to tender when the Act was obtained. Terms were made concerning working arrangements with the OWW which was to operate the line, allowing 20 per cent on net receipts after deducting working expenses.

At the beginning of October a notice appeared in *The Worcestershire Chronicle and Provincial Railway Gazette*[2] mentioning the public meetings and expressing the hope that the new SVR 'stands on a more secure foundation than the last of the name, projected in 1847, the bills for advertising which are, we believe, unpaid to this day, and likely to remain so.'

Mr Whitmore was exceedingly displeased by the decision to take the line up the Severn from Bridgnorth and he strongly supported another railway, the Shrewsbury, Ironbridge &

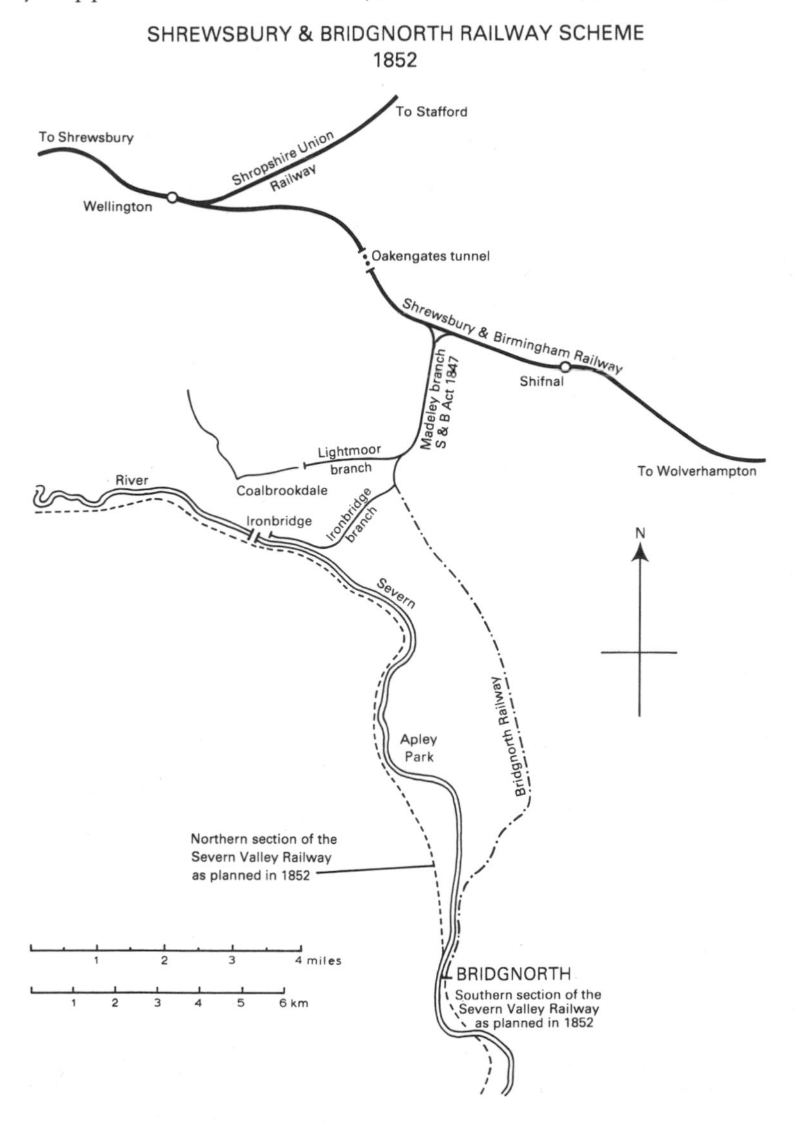

Bridgnorth Railway, known as 'Peele's Line' (probably Joshua John Peele, a prominent Shrewsbury solicitor) from Bridgnorth to the Madeley branch of the S&B. (See map p23) The engineer was Henry Robertson (1816-88), at that time engineer of the S&B and the Madeley branch. The route was closely similar to that originally proposed for the SVR, passing east of Apley Park. A notice of application for an Act appeared on 3 November 1852. The bill was introduced to Parliament by Messrs Clive and Whitmore on 22 February 1853. It did get a second reading, on 11 April, but on 24 June Sir James East reported from the committee on the bills that the preamble had not been proved to their satisfaction and it was thrown out.[3] This left Whitmore determined to fight the SVR by every means in his power. The notice of intended application for an Act to incorporate the SVR Co and to authorise construction of the line was dated 2 November 1852. It outlined the route from a junction with the OWW $5^1/_2$ furlongs south of Hartlebury station, via Hartlebury, Stourport, Wribbenhall, Upper Arley, Highley, Hampton Loade, Bridgnorth, Coalport, Iron Bridge,[4] Buildwas, Cressage and Cound, to terminate by a junction with the Shrewsbury & Chester Railway about 1 mile 1f north of Shrewsbury station. (See map p30) A branch from near Iron Bridge was to serve Coalbrookdale and Madeley, and another from this branch at Lightmoor was to go to Horsehay.

Various features of the route shown on the deposited plan and section are worth mentioning, from south to north. North west of Stourport the line was to cross the Bewdley road and follow the river. It then re-crossed the road and passed through Mount Pleasant in a cutting. At 17 miles 6f, south of Bridgnorth, it crossed the Severn and passed through Bridgnorth Lower Town, then re-crossed the river half a mile north of Bridgnorth bridge. Opposite Apley Park, in an attempt to appease Whitmore, the line was taken away from the Severn through a tunnel of 770yd at a depth of 122ft; after a short space came another tunnel of 228yd and another of 123yd, a total of 1,121yd in less than 3 miles. At Shrewsbury the line had to cross the S&B and the Severn to reach the Shrewsbury & Chester. Nicholson's estimate came to £600,000: £110,000 for land and £490,000 for works. This included £8,500 for the bridge over the Severn at Arley, £8,000 for one near Quatford, £9,000 for one above Bridgnorth and £10,000 for the bridge at Shrewsbury.

The SVR bill was presented in Parliament on 11 February 1853 and was read for the second time and committed on the 16th. It met with considerable opposition from the 'Shrewsbury companies' which caused much delay and additional expense. On 28 March Sir James East reported that the preamble to the bill had been amended, to terminate the main line at a point in Shrewsbury from which it could later be continued to join one of the existing lines and it was recommended that powers for this should be sought in a subsequent session. The powers for branches were to be limited to one line from near Benthall Edge, over the Severn, to a junction with the authorised line of the Wellington & Severn Junction Railway at Madeley. At the board meeting on 26 May 1853 it was resolved to make an agreement with Robert Woodward of Arley Castle to stop trains for him and his family at Arley upon half an hour's notice being given to the stationmaster.

In June a meeting in Kidderminster chaired by the mayor, Mr Kitely, strongly supported moving the junction with the OWW from Hartlebury to Kidderminster, but this was opposed at a subsequent meeting in Stourport. The reason for the Hartlebury connection was, of course, that the SVR was originally intended to connect Shrewsbury and Worcester.[5]

With a few amendments the bill passed the Commons early in July and went before the Select Committee of the Lords. Many people were cross examined before the committee from 5 to 9 August. Various tradesmen in Stourport, Bewdley and Bridgnorth strongly supported the railway. It was stated that the cost of sending freight on the river from Gloucester to Bridgnorth was 10s a ton for 45 miles. By rail this would be 7s - 8s a ton. Thomas Austin Jackson, manager of Eardington ironworks, stated that he used up to 26,000 tons of coal, coke and charcoal per annum. He produced about 6,000 tons of best charcoal iron in a year. He was finding water transport, from Iron Bridge (sic) and to Stourport, was not dependable. The eminent engineer Sir John Hawkshaw gave evidence on 6 August. He had suggested a deviation at Shrewsbury to join the Shrewsbury & Hereford Railway, thereby shortening the line and reducing the estimated cost to £560,000 and this had been adopted. He supported the junction at Hartlebury.

He was followed by Robert Nicholson who spoke at length about the problems and expense created by Mr Whitmore at Apley. The tunnelling would cost much more than a line taken beside the river. He mentioned the Wellington & Severn Junction Railway, at that time before Parliament, as important to the SVR but unsuitable for passenger traffic because of severe gradients, about 1 in 50. Asked if he was familiar with the survey carried out by Robert Stephenson in 1846, he replied that he had been over it in 1847 and 1848 and had completed the survey for the SVR in 1849. It was mentioned that the leading subscribers to the line were prominent railway contractors; Samuel Morton Peto had subscribed between £40,000 and £50,000, Thomas Brassey £30,000, and E.L. Betts whose sum was not stated.

One of the last to be examined was T.C. Whitmore. Besides Apley Park, he also owned considerable property at Bridgnorth and at Chelmarsh near Highley, and was anxious to get a railway to Bridgnorth, but it must not spoil the view from his house. He complained that he would be able to see the railway from his house for three quarters of a mile (how many of us would envy him for that!) and that the ground through which it was to pass was too swampy to support a railway. He did not oppose the line at Chelmarsh - it would improve his property. At Bridgnorth, houses he owned were empty because of the depressed state of the town. Questioned, he admitted the railway would benefit his property there. Why had he not opposed the Stephenson line? Because it was a project of the Shropshire Union whose chairman, Lord Powis, was a friend of his and of his family. He fatuously suggested that not five people would travel from Bridgnorth to Shrewsbury in a month. He thought it 'rather extraordinary' that the people of Bridgnorth preferred the line along the valley rather than the longer route over the top to the Shrewsbury & Birmingham.

John Dixon, a railway contractor working on the S&B Madeley branch, was questioned on borings he had made at Rookery Wood opposite Apley. He spoke of soft clay to a great depth and described the ground as most unsuitable for railway construction. One suspects that his connection with the S&B influenced his statements. This was in fact probed by the examiner. Daniel Fisher, foreman of the SVR boring party, reported that they had found the ground satisfactory.

Henry Robertson, engineer of the S&B and of the 'Peele's Line' supported by Whitmore, described the connection from Bridgnorth to the Madeley branch as best suited to the Shropshire district, again a matter of personal interest.

After all the evidence had been taken the Council made a number of amendments to the bill for the protection of Mr Whitmore; it was reported to the House of Lords on 9 August and received the Royal Assent on the 20th.

CHAPTER 3

Early Years of the SVR Company

The Severn Valley Railway Act of 1853 (c227) incorporated the company and authorised the raising of £600,000 in 30,000 shares of £20 with powers to borrow £200,000 on mortgage. The first directors were named as: George Cecil Weld Forester, Norman Hilton Macdonald, Jonathan Thorp, William Reed, Charles William Tyndale, Francis Parker and Michael Grazebrook. Powers were given to build a railway from a junction with the OWW $5^1/_2$ furlongs south of Hartlebury station and terminating in Shrewsbury in the Parish of Holy Cross and St Giles. A branch was to leave the main line near Benthall Edge to Madeley. Sections 20-2 concerned the passage through Whitmore's estate opposite Apley House, and required the line to be in tunnel between 22 miles and 22 miles 3.11f, as close to the western limits of deviation as possible.

The Wellington & Severn Junction Railway, whose bill was then before Parliament, was to run from the Shrewsbury & Birmingham at Ketley near Wellington to the north bank of the Severn. Section 23 of the SVR Act made it lawful to make a connection between this line and the SVR branch.

At the first board meeting after incorporation, on 1 September 1853, Nicholson's appointment as engineer was confirmed, and on the 19th his salary was fixed at £1,000 per annum plus out-of-pocket expenses up to £200. He was instructed to proceed with the plans before staking out the line. The first general meeting of the SVR shareholders was held

Notes to this chapter will be found on p214.

at the company's office at 31 Parliament Street, Westminster, on 19 September.[1] The chairman, Jonathan Thorp, outlined the advantages which the railway would bring to the districts it served. At Stourport, which had grown rapidly in the past fifty years, over a thousand people worked in ironworks and in the manufacture of worsted and carpets, but progress was hampered by want of a railway which, it was argued, would bring five times as much trade. How this was arrived at was not explained.

Mr Thorp went on to explain that there were 4,000 inhabitants at Bewdley which would yield a large passenger traffic. Bridgnorth was a large town with considerable carpet manufactories, also greatly in need of railway accommodation. At Coalport there was the largest china manufactory in England, second only to one at Paris, employing 700, which imported all materials except coal. Broseley possessed the most extensive concerns manufacturing firebricks and tiles. Both these places promised immense traffic. The Coalbrookdale ironworks employed 4,000 and large quantities of materials were constantly conveyed to and from the works.

He stated that the line, 41 miles long, would join the Shrewsbury & Birmingham Railway. He had no doubt it would be constructed within the estimate of £600,000 and that it would yield a dividend of $7^1/_2$ per cent. Also the OWW had agreed to give them 20 per cent of the receipts from traffic onto their line from the SVR.

At the board meeting on 27 October 1853 it was proposed to deviate the line at Shrewsbury to join the Shrewsbury & Hereford (following Hawkshaw's advice) and to use Shrewsbury Joint station. The S&H was then almost completed; it was to be opened from Ludlow to Hereford on 6 December. A bill for the deviation of 2 miles 11yd was prepared for the 1854 session and Nicholson drew up a plan and section, but before any progress could be made with this the SVR Co was in financial trouble. This was the period, following the Railway Mania, when the raising of capital for new lines was proving difficult, and on 13 February 1854 it was decided that the bill

SVR DEVIATIONS NEAR SHREWSBURY, BRIDGNORTH AND STOURPORT

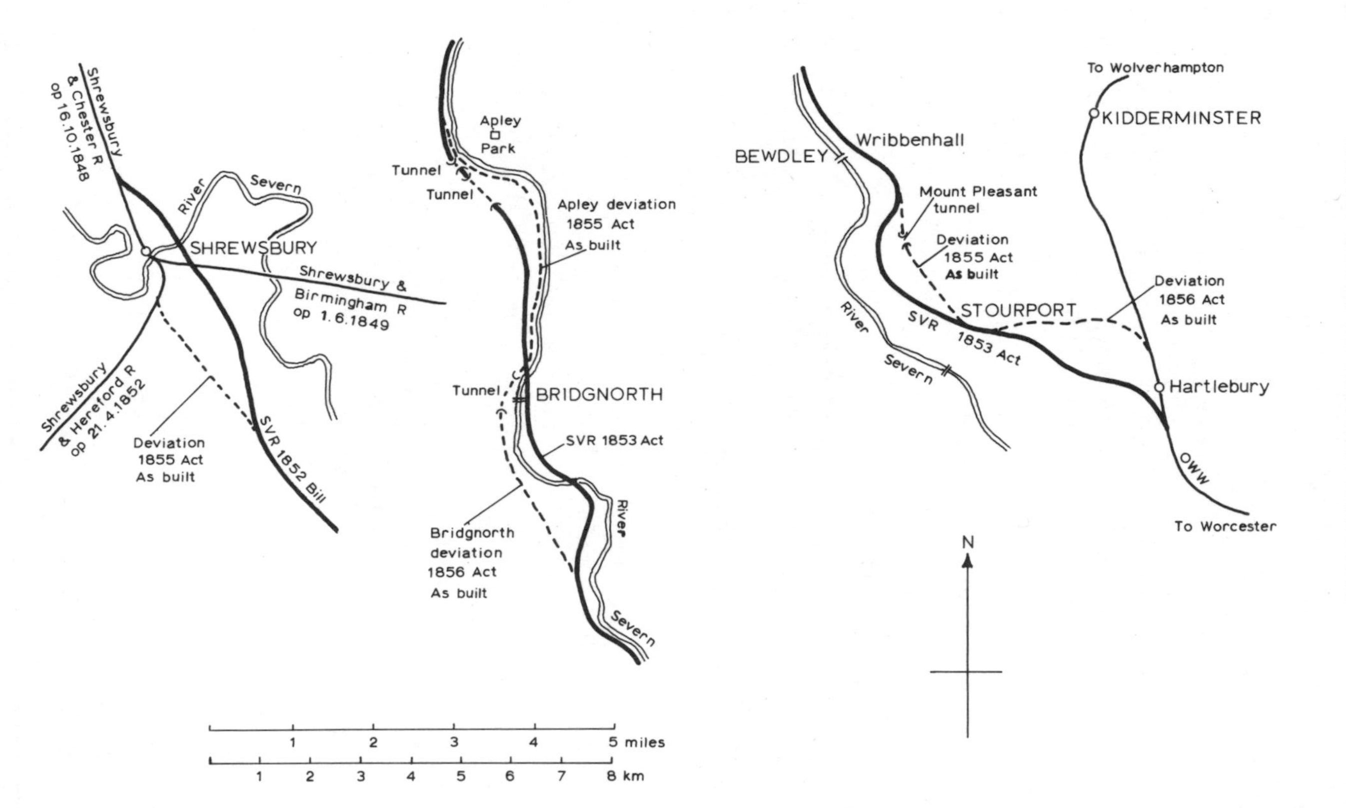
Shrewsbury
& Chester R
op 16.10.1848
River
Severn
SHREWSBURY
Shrewsbury &
Birmingham R
op 1.6.1849
Shrewsbury
& Hereford R
op 21.4.1852
Deviation
1855 Act
As built
SVR 1852 Bill
Apley
Park
Tunnel
Tunnel
Apley deviation
1855 Act
As built
Tunnel
BRIDGNORTH
SVR 1853 Act
River
Bridgnorth
deviation
1856 Act
As built
Severn
To Wolverhampton
KIDDERMINSTER
BEWDLEY
Wribbenhall
Mount Pleasant
tunnel
Deviation
1855 Act
As built
STOURPORT
Deviation
1856 Act
As built
River
SVR
1853 Act
Severn
Hartlebury
OWW
To Worcester
N
1 2 3 4 5 miles
1 2 3 4 5 6 7 8 km

for the Shrewsbury deviation should not be proceeded with beyond the second reading in the Commons without further orders from the board. On 4 April the board was informed that the finance committee had considered the question of reduction of general expenses and had resolved to inform the engineer that the company was not proceeding with the railway, and that his salary must cease for the time being until the company was in a position to proceed with the works. In the meantime he would be paid professional charges for any services. The salary of the secretary, Mr C.E. Reed, was to be reduced from £500 to £300. Mr Peto, who had subscribed heavily to the undertaking, had to be reassured that no money had been wasted. On 19 May he was elected chairman of the board, following the resignation of Jonathan Thorp.

Peto had already been elected, in 1851, chairman of the Chester & Holyhead Railway, an office he held until its amalgamation with the LNWR in 1859, and was at the time engaged in constructing the first military railway, from Balaclava to Sebastopol in the Crimea, which he did without profit or remuneration, for which he was awarded a baronetcy in December 1854. He was re-elected a director of the company at the third meeting of the shareholders on 21 August 1854.

A new parliamentary bill was now being worked out for the 1855 session. The financial affairs of the company were undergoing drastic revision, and Nicholson was preparing deviations from the route in the 1853 Act. These were: one of 2 miles 152yd between Stourport and Bewdley, in which the line remained east of the road and passed through a tunnel of 120yd under Mount Pleasant at a depth of 85ft 6in; Apley deviation 3 miles 7f 100yd taking the line beside the river and so avoiding the tunnels; and the deviation at Shrewsbury to join the S&H at what would be known as Sutton Bridge Junction. (See map p30)

Needless to say, arch-enemy Whitmore was up in arms again. It was suggested that Whitmore should receive £15,000 compensation and £150 per acre for land purchased by the company. Nicholson was asked on 17 July 1854 to see what arrangement he could make. The new plans and sections were prepared and deposited on 30 November 1854.

The next setback for the company occurred on 9 May 1855 when the engineer, Robert Nicholson, died at his home in Newcastle at the early age of 46. Besides the SVR, he had also been working on the Border Counties Railway which was about to be started. He had been in London giving evidence on the Liverpool Waterworks bill and while there he caught a cold which developed into a serious illness.[2] Probably, like several of his contemporaries, he was weakened by overwork. John Fowler was appointed to replace him. Born at Sheffield in 1817, he was at the time only 38 years old and was later to achieve distinction as engineer of the Metropolitan Railway and, with Benjamin Baker, of the Forth Bridge.

Sir Morton Peto chaired a special meeting of the shareholders on 16 June 1855 to approve the new bill for reducing the capital of the company by about a third and to authorise the deviations. He stated that the cost of the line was reduced from £17,000 to £12,000 per mile, for a double line of rails, and he was confident it would yield about 8 per cent.[3]

In presenting evidence before the house of Lords Committee on 12 July, Henry Whitmore, being examined on behalf of his brother Thomas, stated that his brother was satisfied with the arrangement made by the SVR and that his objections were removed. Fowler stated that although the Apley deviation was 23 chains, or over a quarter of a mile longer, it resulted in a saving of £47,000. The original tunnel line would have cost £74,000 and the substituted line by the river would be £27,000. He added that this, together with cutting out the Horsehay and Madeley branches, made a total saving of about £120,000, cutting the total estimate from £600,000 to £480,000.[4]

Thomas Whitmore was so satisfied that when the railway was built he cut down some fine trees to give him a better view of the trains,[5] but he was able to enjoy them for only three years, because he died at Apley on 13 March 1865 aged only 58. Two years later the estate was sold to William Orme Foster, the Stourbridge ironmaster.

The SVR bill received the Royal Assent on 30 July 1855. The new Act c 183 repealed the 1853 Act but the company was to continue incorporated. The share capital was reduced to £48,000 in 24,000 shares of £20, with power to borrow £160,000 on mortgage. The three deviations were authorised, and five years were allowed for completion of the railway. Sections 52 and 76 concerned exchange of traffic with the Wellington & Severn Junction Railway. Section 77 confirmed running powers over the S&H between the junction and Shrewsbury station and Section 80 ruled that the S&H, GWR, LNWR and Shropshire Union were to make all arrangements for the accommodation of the SVR at Shrewsbury Station.

It will be noted that the line was still to start from a junction with the OWW south of Hartlebury station and that it was to pass through Bridgnorth Low Town with two crossings of the Severn below and above Bridgnorth. The mayor of Bridgnorth wrote on 16 August to the SVR chairman stating that it was the wish of influential inhabitants that a deviation should be made at Bridgnorth and the position of the station should be changed. Fowler was instructed to prepare rough plans and sections of the changes. What these were is not known, but by November further plans and sections had been prepared for another bill to authorise two more deviations: the first from a junction north of Hartlebury station and passing round the north of Hartlebury Castle to join the authorised line at Upper Mitton, north of Stourport, 2 miles 6.22f; the second, at Bridgnorth, from near Eardington ironworks, over a viaduct at Oldbury, round the eastern side of Pan Pudding Hill, through a tunnel of 500yd (actually it became 550yd) at a depth of 95ft 6in under the High Town, regaining the authorised line just beyond Bridgnorth at the south end of the Apley deviation, 4 miles 1.57f. The first shortened the line at the south end and avoided the need for a second station at Hartlebury, and the second, while involving a tunnel under Bridgnorth, eliminated two bridges over the Severn thereby saving £8,000 at Quatford and £9,000 above Bridgnorth. The shortening of the line at Shrewsbury had already saved £10,000 on another bridge over the Severn.

By way of stimulating support for the SVR Sir Morton Peto addressed public meetings at Bridgnorth, Bewdley, Stourport and other places on the route during March and April 1856. The result was a considerable increase in the number of shares taken up.[6] At another public meeting in Ironbridge on 1 July Peto said that £150,000 must be raised before work could start on the railway, and of this nearly £70,000 had been subscribed. Under Fowler great improvements had been made in the line, and a new bill before Parliament had passed the Commons. He still predicted a double line, at a cost of under £15,000 a mile. The construction was to be under a guaranteed contract, the contractor to carry all risks. He did not say, of course, that he expected to be the contractor. A dividend of 7½ per cent was expected. T.A. Jackson, agent of W.O. Foster of Stourton Castle and manager of Eardington ironworks stressed his need for the railway. About three years earlier they had a vessel laden at Montford Bridge on the Severn above Shrewsbury for thirteen months before they could get it to Eardington, because of the state of the river. This compelled them to keep a much larger stock of charcoal, valued at £40,000, instead of £10,000.

The SVR Act of 21 July 1856 c 111 authorised the deviations and granted a further two years for compulsory purchase of lands. Nine days later Fowler reported that he had arranged with Mr Whitmore the exact course of the line through his property to the satisfaction of Mr Whitmore and the SVR Co. A new threat now appeared in the form of a LNWR bill for a branch from the SU near Wellington to Coalport. On 28 January 1857 the SVR board resolved to oppose it.

Some curious business now began to take place. On 10 July 1857 it was resolved that a tender for the works by Smith & Knight should be accepted. No details of the tender have been found. This brought forth the following letter from Sir Morton Peto, dated 28 July:

Gentlemen,

As it is now necessary that arrangements should be made for the construction of your Line it is essential that I should rightly understand the position in which I am placed with the Company.

It will no doubt be in your recollection that when this undertaking was first established I and my friends agreed to take Shares to the Amount of £225,000. 0s 0d upon the understanding that my friends were to be the Contractors for the works at prices to be arranged with the Company's Engineer. At a subsequent period it was unfortunately discovered that the Company's finances were in a very unsatisfactory state owing to a variety of names having been put down in the list of Subscribers of persons who were not competent to fulfil their engagements. At this crisis I entered into the Direction and was placed in the Chair of the Company with a view to set matters to rights, and I am happy to think that since that period the exertions of myself and my colleagues have been attended with beneficial results.

My continuance in the Direction would of course be inconsistent with my being interested in the Contract, and I think it, therefore, right to notify you that I am prepared to retain the Interests in the Company for which I have subscribed, and to take the Contracts for the Works as originally intended, provided the Company feel themselves in a situation to provide the additional funds requisite for carrying out the Undertaking.

With a view therefore to their entering upon this question I think it right now to retire from the Direction, and beg you will consider this Letter as an intimation of my Resignation.

Whenever the Directors are prepared to enter upon the subject I shall be ready to agree to the terms of a Contract for the construction of the Works upon being satisfied that the necessary Funds will be forthcoming on the part of the Company.

I am Gentlemen
Your very abdt servt
S. Morton Peto

Peto's resignation was accepted by the board. The company was having severe difficulties in raising the money necessary to begin the works. Two new bills were prepared for the next session of Parliament: the first to extend the time to purchase the land and to carry out the works; the second to abandon the undertaking.

In the meantime, on 27 July, the LNWR had absorbed the Shropshire Union Railways & Canal and had been authorised to construct the branch from near Wellington to Coalport. Having failed in its opposition to this measure the SVR now instructed Fowler to prepare plans for a connecting line of 5.45 furlongs from a south-facing junction with the SVR, to cross the Severn to a junction with the LNWR. In other words, if you can't beat them, join them! On the advice of Sir Morton Peto, the decision on whether to promote the bill for extension of time or for abandonment was to be left until the next half yearly meeting in February 1858.

On the assumption that the work would go ahead, Peto, Brassey & Betts prepared to tender for the contract to construct the railway according to Fowler's specifications. Three suggestions were put forward: (1) to build a double-track railway for £469,740; (2) to build all works for double track, but with a single line of rails for £389,690; (3) to prepare earthworks for two-thirds of the length, and tunnels, for single line; and underbridges, other than viaducts and bridges over streams, for single line with foundations for double line for £363,690. These prices included stations up to a cost of £22,500; if stations amounted to less, the difference was to be deducted from the contract price.

On 20 February 1858 the directors decided on the third choice and the tender was accepted, subject to the sanction of the shareholders, for completion of a single line and stations by the end of 1859. At the shareholders' meeting on 26 February, chaired by Col Forester, the secretary, Mr C. Reed, reported that the subscribed capital of the company had been reduced to £480,000 and borrowing power to £160,000, a total of £640,000. The subscribed capital was held by residents on the line, by shareholders in lines joining the SVR, and by the general public. The board has ascertained that the cost of land, parliamentary matters, engineering and office expenses would be covered by £70,000.

The tender of the contractors assumed that they would accept payment to the extent of £240,000 in shares at par. Borrowing powers of the company would raise £160,000 leaving the general body of shareholders to pay only £13,000, making a total of £530,000, or £13,000 a mile. It was stated that when the SVR or any part of it was built the OWW would undertake to maintain and work it for five years and to pay rates and taxes and government duty and to provide all engines and carriages for half the gross receipts, and to allow the company 10 per cent of the profits. Working drawings were ready, much of the land had been bought and the remainder was under contract and construction could be started in two months. The directors therefore recommended that the abandonment bill which was before Parliament should be withdrawn and the bill for extension of time should be prosecuted, that the tender of Peto, Brassey & Betts should be accepted and construction started. These recommendations were adopted at a special meeting immediately afterwards.

On 10 March the board accepted the tender of Fuller & Whithall, £2,150, for negotiating purchase of land at £86,000 plus £14,000 to Mr Whitmore. Fowler attended the meeting on 21 April and proposed to accept £16,000 for all past and future services until the completion of the main line. This was accepted. The contract for the works was sealed on 26 May. The bill for extension of time passed through Parliament without amendment. The Act, on 23 July 1858 c 135, extended the period for completion to 23 July 1861. The bill for the Coalport Junction line was not proceeded with; the LNWR completed its branch which was opened on 17 June 1861, so becoming the first 'main line' railway into that part of the valley.

All was now set for going ahead with construction of the SVR. It was to be single track but it was agreed to pay an extra £26,000 for which the contractors would build earthworks for double track. The contract[8] stated that the railway was to be constructed on the pattern of the Mid Kent Railway. This line, also engineered by John Fowler and authorised by Act of 1855, ran from Lewisham on the North Kent line to Beckenham on the Farnborough extension of the West End & Crystal Palace Railway. It was opened on 1 January 1857. A clause in the contract maintained the SVR company's power to elect to have the works made for double line, for £389,690. If the company required more expensive bridges under sections 35-7 of the 1853 Act, it was to bear the additional expense.

Fowler's specification, appended to the contract, gave minute details of fencing. Cuttings and embankments were to be 30ft wide at formation level which would be 20in below rail level at the centre and 2ft below at the sides. Rails were to weigh 70lb per yard and chairs were to weigh 21lb each. Sleepers of 'best Memel or Dantzic timber' were to be not less than 8ft 6in long and 9 x $4^1/_2$in in section. Tunnels were to be 24ft wide and not less than 16ft high at the centre of each line of rails. This clearly referred to double-line tunnels. The contractor was to be prepared to line them with brickwork if the engineer decided this was necessary. The Bridgnorth tunnel was to be built without shafts, and without disturbing any buildings. Payment to the contractors was to be made monthly on Fowler's certificates to the full amount of work carried out, but ten per cent was to be retained 'for due performance' up to a total amount of £20,000. So, five years after its Act of Incorporation, the SVR company could at last look forward to seeing its railway constructed.

CHAPTER 4

Building the Railway

Construction of the railway began in the summer of 1858. The resident engineer was Fowler's assistant, Henry Orlando Bridgeman, born at Blymhill in Staffordshire on 26 January 1825. His father, the Rev Henry Edmund Bridgeman, at that time rector of Blymhill, was the fourth son of Orlando Bridgeman, created Viscount Newport and first Earl of Bradford in 1815. Bridgeman had worked under Fowler from 1848, first as resident engineer on the Manchester, Sheffield & Lincolnshire Railway Leverton - Lincoln extension, then on various other lines including the Worcester - Hereford. From 1852 to 1856 he was acting engineer on the London, Tilbury & Southend Railway, and before coming to the SVR he had spent two years surveying a railway in Algeria. He took full charge of the construction works on the SVR until its completion in 1861, after which he spent his time assisting Bidder on various foreign railway projects until his untimely death in 1879 at the age of 54.[1]

Fowler's reports at the shareholders' meetings give us a good idea of progress. On 9 August 1858 he said that the contractors were in possession of nearly $2^1/_2$ miles of land at Stourport, Highley, Chelmarsh, Bridgnorth and Broseley, and works on some of the heaviest portions were in progress. The cutting through the sandstone at the north end of Bridgnorth tunnel was begun and the viaduct over the Stour between Hartlebury and Stourport, and several large bridges were to be started immediately. Materials had been sent by river to

Notes to this chapter are on p214.

Ironbridge, Bridgnorth, Arley and Stourport and as soon as the land was available work would start.

So as to make better use of the Severn for the transport of materials, an iron steam tug was built at Shrewsbury by Edward Jeffreys, the locomotive superintendent of the Shrewsbury & Hereford Railway at Coleham, Shrewsbury. The tug was 44ft long with a 6ft beam and had a draft of 15 to 16in. It was driven by two paddles which could be reversed independently of each other, and it had a rudder at each end. It was intended for towing barges between Shrewsbury and Gloucester. It was launched on 4 September 1858 and was named *Christiana*.[2] No further information about this vessel has been found. How Jeffreys came to construct it is not known, though from 1 July 1853 Thomas Brassey was in charge of working the S&H under a nine-year lease. As Brassey was also contractor of the SVR he may have instructed his locomotive superintendent to build the steam tug.

Although an agreement with the contractors to build the railway as a single line but with earthworks for double, for an extra £26,000, was confirmed on 31 December 1858, it was decided later to defer the additional expenditure until traffic on the line made double track indispensable.[3] As it turned out, over-bridges, masonry under-bridges and viaducts were built for double track, but the two tunnels, although of generous dimensions, were for single track. The short Knowle Sands tunnel is classed as an over-bridge.

At the next half-yearly meeting on 23 February 1859 the secretary reported that about 20 miles of land between Hartlebury and Bridgnorth had been given to the contractors and in a few more weeks they would have all the land. It was hoped that the remaining land to Shrewsbury would be available during the spring. Fowler reported that seven cuttings were completed and fourteen more were in progress, as also were ten bridges and the Stour viaduct. Nearly 12 miles of rails and permanent way material had been delivered and, depending on the availability of land, the line should be opened for traffic by 1 October 1860. On 18 May 1859 the law clerk reported that the contractors were now in possession of the whole of the land between Hartlebury and Bridgnorth, except Mr Whitmore's lands at Chelmarsh. North of here Lord Berwick's land had been paid for and satisfactory progress was being made with other landowners.

About 2 miles from Hartlebury the railway had to be cut through a sandstone ridge in a cutting a third of a mile long and 60ft deep. This proved one of the heaviest pieces of excavation on the line. It would have been easier to tunnel it, but this would have yielded insufficient spoil for the embankment in the Stour valley beyond. The method of excavation was most unusual. A tunnel was, in fact, bored through the hard sandstone at railway level from several shafts, and a line of rails was laid through. A train of wagons was run in and the wagons, one at a time, were positioned under a shaft. At a given signal from below navvies threw spoil down the shaft. When the wagon was full another signal was given, the next wagon was put in position, and so the work continued. In this way all the softer upper material was excavated, without having to lift it into wagons. The hard rock beneath was finally blasted with gunpowder.[4] A minor road, Wilden Top Road, was carried over the cutting on a high segmental arch.

Beyond here the line crossed the Stour by a large skew segmental arch flanked by another arch on the east side and three on the west, on the square. Near Upper Mitton another minor road was crossed by a brick viaduct of three semi-circular arches.

Two new bills were before Parliament at that time: the Tenbury Railway from Woofferton on the Shrewsbury & Hereford to Tenbury, and the Much Wenlock & Severn Junction which would join the SVR near Buildwas. Both bills received the support of the SVR and were given the Royal Assent on 21 July 1859. The Much Wenlock line was expected to bring considerable limestone traffic onto the SVR, and the Tenbury Railway was seen as part of a line to Bewdley, already being planned, which would form a route to South Wales.

By 8 August Fowler was able to report that over 350,000yd^3

of excavation had been removed and twenty large bridges and viaducts were in hand or completed. The tunnels at Mount Pleasant and Bridgnorth were begun and foundations for the Severn bridge were in progress. Unstable ground had caused trouble with slips in several places, a problem which was to continue on the SVR, and about $^1/_2$ mile north of the Highley station site it had been necessary to deviate from the originally planned course of the railway. This involved a considerable change in the character of the works, and was expected to delay the opening, probably to about the end of 1860.[5]

Work was now proceeding on the viaducts near Bewdley. *Berrows Worcester Journal* reported on 11 June 1859 that the scaffolding was erected for the bridge over the road at Wribbenhall and on 25 June there appeared this description of the works:

> Bewdley: Works on the Severn Valley Railway are proceeding with almost unparalleled rapidity in this neighbourhood. For some time past the destruction of the houses in Wribbenhall has given the place an appearance somewhat resembling a town that has been sacked by an invading army. Out of this seeming destruction, however, may be expected shortly to arise as beautiful a structure as any on the whole line of the railway. On Saturday last (18 June) the first stones of the viaduct that crosses the main turnpike road were laid, the one by the mayor of Bewdley, John Nicholls Esq, and the other by John Montgomery Esq MD. From the designs of the bridge, which will be on a skew arch, and the elaborate workmanship of the entire structure, it cannot fail of being a great ornament to this place in an artistic point of view.

The bridge, built of massive sandstone blocks, must have been heavy work, for it was not until Saturday 10 December that the keystones of the main arch were laid, one by James Tart, then mayor of Bewdley, assisted by Edward

Bryan, and other by William Field.[6] Mr Tart named the viaduct 'Bewdley Bridge' as if there were not one already over the Severn.

On Thursday 24 November 1859 the contractors arranged a ceremony for the laying of the foundation stone of the bridge over the Severn which took place at 3.00pm. Miles Day, on behalf of the contractors, presented an inscribed silver trowel to Mr Bridgeman who then laid the stone, after which he named the bridge 'Victoria Bridge' in honour of the sovereign. Beneath the stone a glass bottle was deposited containing silver and copper coins and a paper signed by the principal persons on which was written:

> The foundation stone of this bridge was laid by Henry Orlando Bridgman (sic) Esq., C.E., resident engineer, on the 24th day of November, in the year of our Lord, One Thousand Eight Hundred and Fifty Nine, and the twenty third year of the Reign of her Majesty, Queen Victoria.
>
> The arch of the bridge is to be constructed principally of cast iron - 200 feet span - and up to the present time, will be the largest cast-iron arch constructed in these kingdoms. John Fowler Esq., engineer-in-chief, London. Messrs. Brassey, Peto, and Betts, contractors, also of London.
>
> The railway works were commenced in the autumn of 1858, and are expected to be completed in the spring of 1861. The railway commences at Shrewsbury, and terminates at the Hartlebury Station of the Oxford, Worcester and Wolverhampton Railway, a distance of 40 miles.'

Fowler reported on 8 February 1860 that the contractors were in possession of $34^1/_2$ miles of land and, despite the long wet weather which had caused numerous slips, work had gone ahead. Between Hartlebury and Bridgnorth, where there were the heaviest works, over 9 miles of formation was ready for the permanent way. The principal cuttings remaining unfinished were: 2 miles from Hartlebury, at Arley, and north of

Highley where the large slip had occurred resulting in a deviation. Between Bridgnorth and Shrewsbury the earthworks were lighter. Altogether over 800,000yd^3 of earth had been moved. Mount Pleasant tunnel was begun, the heading was through, and for about 80 out of 123yd it was excavated to its full size, and three lengths of brickwork were completed. The Bridgnorth tunnel was likewise in a forward state. Of the bridges, six public road bridges and three viaducts were completed and eighteen stream and occupation bridges were well in hand. Good progress had been made with the masonry of the foundations of the Severn bridge and the contractors had entrusted the Coalbrookdale Co with the castings and wrought-iron work of the superstructure. Permanent way was laid and ballasted for 5 miles and large quantities of permanent way material were on the ground or in course of delivery. Plans of the station buildings were prepared and would soon be with the contractors. The Much Wenlock line was to be proceeded with so as to be opened at the same time as the SVR line. The law clerk reported on 29 March that the whole of Whitmore's land required by the railway was now in the hands of the contractors.

A meeting was held on 5 April 1860 to consider two bills before Parliament; the first to enable the OWW Co to take on lease the SVR undertaking, and the second for a railway from Tenbury to the SVR near Bewdley. In the first bill the SVR Co was to grant a lease of the undertaking to the OWW Co for 999 years. The OWW Co was to work the SVR and to pay 55 per cent of gross earnings from SVR traffic on the present or future OWW system. The SVR (Leasing) Act which came into effect on 14 June 1860 c 76 confirmed the above arrangements and gave power to the OWW Co to purchase the SVR at par within ten years. The OWW Co retained its original title for only two more days, for by the West Midland Railway Act of 16 June 1860 c 81, which authorised the amalgamation of the Newport, Abergavenny & Hereford and Worcester & Hereford railway companies with the OWW, its title became the West Midland Railway Company.

The Tenbury, Bewdley, Kidderminster & Worcester Junction Railway was projected in 1859 in connection with a link proposed by the SVR from Bewdley to the OWW at Kidderminster. The SVR undertook to contribute £7,000 and the OWW £1,000 towards its construction. With its name shortened to the Tenbury & Bewdley Railway, its Act was passed in 1860 (see chapter 5). At the board meeting on 20 June the first mention was made of a railway between Bridgnorth and Wolverhampton, to be dealt with in chapter 7.

Although trouble was being experienced with landslips because of continuous wet weather for several months, by 1 August 1860 Fowler was able to report that about 12 miles of permanent way had been laid and that nearly all the materials for the remainder of the line had been delivered on the site. It was still confidently expected that the section from Hartlebury to Bewdley would be open on 1 November and that the northern portion would be completed by May 1861. The station buildings were in hand and would be ready in time for the opening. The capital account showed that by 30 June £327,934 had been received and £320,525 had been spent, leaving a balance of £7,409[7].

In his next report, on 2 February 1861, Fowler stated that the works on the railway were beginning to assume a more finished appearance; 35 miles of cuttings and embankments were completed, so were the tunnels except for the fronts, and most of the bridges were finished. The abutments of the bridge over the Severn were built and the castings and forgings were being fitted together in the contractor's yard at Coalbrookdale; erection of the arch was to start that month and was expected to be completed in June. About 21 miles of permanent way were laid and ballasted. Work on the station buildings had been delayed by the wet weather in the autumn and the recent severe frost, but they would be completed before the opening of the line which was expected before August.

The wet weather had certainly caused several severe slips

along the line.[8] Early in 1861 the stone wall beside the road in Wribbenhall just north of the viaduct collapsed, taking two men with it, but they were not seriously hurt. About 2 miles above here at Folly Point, where the line is close to the river, about two acres of woodland slipped into the river, carrying down several large trees. At a place called 'The Wren's Nest' near Linley several acres of land and underwood became separated and started moving down into the river in the summer of 1861. The weight of the railway embankment and the pressure from behind lifted up the bed of the river until it became dry land, and forced the water into a narrow channel opposite. At Chestnut Coppice opposite Apley another slip occurred in June.[9]

At the half-yearly meeting on 6 February 1861 mention was made of the promised connecting line from Bewdley to Kidderminster, to form a through route between Kidderminster and the Shrewsbury & Hereford Railway at Woofferton via Bewdley and Tenbury. This was authorised in the West Midland and Severn Valley Companies' Act of 1 August 1861 c 212. Details of this important connection will be given in chapter 5.

An interesting aspect of the SVR works is brought to light in the 1861 Census. In a chapter titled 'Shropshire Navvies; the Builders of the Severn Valley Railway'.,[10] Iris L. Harris tabulates information from the census return about the men who built the railway. Altogether 741 men were listed as working on the railway within Shropshire; of these 206 (27.9 per cent) came from Shropshire; 170 (22.9 per cent) from Ireland; 98 (13.2 per cent) from Staffordshire, Worcestershire, Herefordshire and Warwickshire; 53 (7.2 per cent) from East Midlands counties and the remainder from various parts of England, Wales (21) and Scotland (4). Their ages ranged from under 15 (7) to over 60 (14). Most of them (416) were aged from 20 to 34 and another 204 were 35 to 49. Of the total 258 were married, 442 unmarried, 20 were widowers and 21 unknown. There were 207 living with wife and children (if any), in Shrewsbury, Ironbridge Gorge and Bridgnorth; 245

were listed as 'heads of households', 313 were lodging in other people's homes, and 123 in inns and licensed lodging houses. Sixty lived in 'temporary or makeshift accommodation' which consisted of turf and mud huts, caves or old lime kilns etc. These examples are in Shropshire only, in which over three quarters of the SVR lay. One could reasonably assume that the navvies on the 10 miles in Worcestershire would be divided in roughly the same proportions.

Various incidents were reported in *Berrow's Worcester Journal.* On 8 July 1859 David Deer, one of the gangers employed on the SVR at Upper Arley, made off with the whole of the wages due to about twelve or fifteen men for two weeks' work 'leaving the poor fellows and their families destitute.' Accidents were common. A labourer at work in Mount Pleasant tunnel on 23 January 1860 lost an eye and part of his nose when a large piece of timber fell on him. A year later, on 9 January 1861, in the cutting south of the tunnel another labourer, James Bishop, was killed when a blast hurled rocks at his head. The ganger was instructed in future to ensure that men were withdrawn to a safe distance before blasting. It seems extraordinary that such an instruction should be necessary. In the same place three weeks later another navvy was injured when a quantity of earth and stones fell onto him. On 9 March a navvy was injured in the cutting south of the Victoria Bridge when a 20 lb clod of earth fell on him from a height of 20 - 40ft. He was taken to Bewdley in a fishing boat 'and immediately placed under the care of Dr Webster.' A few days later a navvy was almost killed in the cutting at Arley when three wagon loads of earth fell on him.

Geologists were not slow to take advantage of the exposure of rocks in the cuttings, and following publication of an article in *Geologist Magazine* in December 1860 a group from Bewdley visited the cutting south east of the Victoria Bridge where they examined exposed coal measures and other sedimentary deposits and found fossil remains of coal plants.[11] This is a cutting where numerous slips have occurred and much of it is strengthened by walling and rubble, so that little can now be seen of the original rocks. They are also covered by plant growth and soil.

On 11 May 1861 the first locomotive with a train of twelve ballast wagons passed through Wribbenhall. For many inhabitants it was the first train they had seen. The previous day the fourth and last of the ribs of the Victoria Bridge had been completed and it was expected that the bridge would be finished in about six weeks.[12] This is the largest structure on the line. The main span of 200ft consists of four ribs with a rise of 20ft each built up of nine cast-iron segments of '**I**' section, 4ft deep at the centre increasing to 4ft 9in at the springing, each weighing 7 tons, and tested under a load of 75 tons. They are securely bound together by wrought-iron bracing. The radius of the lower flange of the ribs in 260ft. The total weight of iron is about 500 tons.[13] The top three segments on each side are inscribed 'Messrs Brassey & Co Contractors', 'Victoria Bridge 1861 / John Fowler Engineer', and 'Cast and erected by the Coalbrookdale Company'. At each end is a segmental arch of 30ft span turned in twelve rings of blue bricks. At the north-west end a tow path was built beside the river. No inscribed foundation stone is visible anywhere, so it is not possible to check the spelling of Bridgeman on it. It has perhaps become buried.

On 5 August 1861 Fowler reported that, except for the slippery places, the earthworks were nearly finished. Tunnels and bridges were almost completed and only about 3 miles of permanent way remained to be laid. Stations were finished except for fittings and furnishings. The telegraph line was in progress and signalling (albeit rudimentary) was in a forward state. He had minutely examined the line with Mr Brassey and he considered it should be possible to open it in October 1861.

As things turned out, he was over optimistic; the slips proved more troublesome than expected and it was the end of 1861 before the line was ready for inspection. This was carried out for the Board of Trade by Col William Yolland, and his report is dated 30 December 1861.[14] In it he gave a detailed account of the railway and its various structures, but he listed several matters which required attention before he would recommend opening for public traffic. He required a turntable to be installed at Hartlebury and completion of the one at Buildwas; indicators were required at nearly all the facing points on the main line and some of the points were to be set or weighted differently. He suggested a different layout at Buildwas station, because of the gradients, recommending doubling of the SVR for a short length and making a double junction with the Wenlock Railway, and a safety siding. He was concerned about a level crossing on a minor road near Hartlebury which had not been sanctioned by Parliament.

His comments on the signalling shed some light on early operating methods. He complained that many of the distant signals could not be seen from the platforms, because of the nature of the line. Fowler stated that they had not been able to make the distant and the intermediate or repeating signals work properly, to ensure that the distant signal was on when the repeating signal was on. The term 'distant signal' clearly had a different meaning in 1861. Yolland blamed the person who had erected the signals.

Because of these shortcomings and the incompleteness of various works he withheld permission for opening. Fowler soon had these matters attended to and Yolland made another inspection on 15 January 1862. He was pleased to note that an undertaking had been given to apply for parliamentary sanction to maintain the level crossing near Hartlebury - it was granted in the SVR Act 30 June 1864 (ch 151). The improvements at Buildwas were being undertaken, with a second platform on the main line. The signalling had been made to work in accordance with his requirements. In every other respect he was satisfied and in his report dated 23 January 1862[15] he recommended the Board of Trade to sanction opening. On 17 January two trains ran over the line, calling at the stations with apparatus for working it.[16]

The formal opening took place on 31 January. The special train of twenty-two coaches left Worcester Shrub Hill station at 11.30. Passengers included Lord Shelbourne, chairman of the GWR; Col Forester, Chairman of the SVR; A.C. Sherriff, general manager of the West Midland Railway; John Fowler and H.O. Bridgeman, engineers; Messrs Brassey and Field, contractors; J. Pritchard MP; the mayors of Bewdley and Kidderminster, and various railway directors. At stations along the line the numbers were increased and at Bridgnorth the train was joined by the Bridgnorth Rifle Band. It arrived at Shrewsbury at 14.00. While there an extra engine and three more coaches were added, and at 14.20 it returned non-stop to Bridgnorth where it arrived at 15.15. Here there was a public dinner at the new Assembly Room, followed by numerous speeches and toasts.[17]

Public services operated by the WMR began the following day, 1 February, as shown on the accompanying timetable. On the same day the Wenlock & Severn Junction Railway was opened from the SVR at Buildwas to Much Wenlock.

At the half-yearly meeting on 15 March it was stated that the total receipts of the company amounted to £523,396 and total expenditure £521,098, leaving a balance of £2,298. In his last report dated 19 February Fowler stated that the opening had been delayed by the numerous and large slips in various places, but that by means of proper drainage and continued attention the works were in a perfectly safe and satisfactory condition. He ended by stating: 'It is due to Mr Brassey to state, that through great difficulties, and at considerable expense to himself he has finished the works and permanent way to my entire satisfaction, and the trains of the West Midland Co have been run with great regularity.'

In accordance with the contract, payment was made to the contractors for the full amount of work completed each month. A total of thirty five payments were made, amounting to a total of £325,398 9s 7d. Of this £240,000 was in the form of shares in the SVR Co and the remainder was in cash. Payments were as follows:

Payments to Peto, Brassey & Betts by John Fowler for construction of the SVR

	£		£
1	9,500 to 31.12.1858	19	15,000 to 1.9.1860
2	11,000 to 1.3.1859	20	5,000 to 1.10.1860
3	10,500 to 20.4.1859	21	9,000 to 1.11.1860
4	11,000 to 1.6.1859	22	13,000 to 1.12.1860
5	12,000 to 1.7.1859	23	6,000 to 1.1.1861
6	9,500 to 1.8.1859	24	8,000 to 1.2.1861
7	27 200 to 1.10.1859	25	7,000 to 1.3.1861
8	9,000 to 1.11.1859	26	11,000 to 1.4.1861
9	7,500 to 1.12.1859	27	11,000 to 1.5.1861
10	16,000 to 1.1.1860	28	11,000 to 1.6.1861
11	12,000 to 1.2.1860	29	13,000 to 1.7.1861
12	17,000 to 1.31860	30	8,000 to 1.8.1861
13	14,000 to 1.4.1860	31	16,500 to 1.9.1861
14	9,000 to 1.5.1860	32	4,000 to 1.10.1861
15	8,000 to 1.6.1860	33	20,000 to 31.10.1861
16	10,000 to 1.7.1860	34	6,000 to 31.12.1861
17	20,000 to 1.8.1860	35	30,000 to 1.11.1862
18	13,000 to 7.8.1860		

Final Certificate: Balance of £5,198 9s 7d paid 2.2.1864

The SVR remained primarily a local line. As a route from Shrewsbury to London it was the longest and slowest. Distances were as follows:

Shrewsbury to Paddington via Worcester and Oxford	172½ miles
Shrewsbury to Paddington via Birmingham and Oxford	171½ miles
Shrewsbury to Paddington via Birmingham and High Wycombe (after 1910)	152¾ miles
Shrewsbury to Euston via Stafford and Nuneaton	162¾ miles
Shrewsbury to Euston via Wolverhampton LL - HL and Birmingham New Street	155½ miles

From 4 March 1969 when the Shrewsbury trains were switched from Wolverhampton Low Level to High Level the last has been the only route.

CHAPTER 5

The Railway Becomes Established

At the SVR half-yearly meeting on 20 August 1862 the deputy chairman stated that 'the line was opened on 1 February in a very incomplete state, with scarcely a single siding into any one mineral work of Coalbrookdale or Broseley, commonly called the Shropshire mineral district, and without access to the limestone for which Wenlock is so celebrated. Already we have it from the chairman of the West Midland Co that the mileage receipt has risen from £6 per mile in a week in February to £16 in July.' He predicted a good future.

Under the terms of the West Midland & Severn Valley Railways Act of 29 July 1862 c183 the WM Co had to pay rent to the SVR shareholders half-yearly, preference shareholders receiving 4½ per cent, and ordinary shareholders 3 per cent rising to 4½ per cent by 1868. The GWR was to purchase the SVR on or before 31 December 1871. But only one year later the WMR was dissolved, after 1 August 1863, when it became a part of the GWR Co[1] and from that time the SVR was known as the Severn Railway branch of the GWR.

Except at its ends, the only railway with which the SVR made direct connection was the branch from Buildwas to Much Wenlock. This climbed away from Buildwas at 1 in 48 and reached Much Wenlock on gradients of 1 in 40, 45 and 48, climbing a total of 352ft in 3 miles. As on the SVR, John Fowler was chief engineer. It was built by the Much Wenlock & Severn Junction Railway Co incorporated in 1859.[2] At Buildwas an extension passed under the SVR and terminated at a wharf

Notes to this chapter are on p215

WEST MIDLAND RAILWAY.

TIME TABLE
FOR
SEVERN VALLEY BRANCH.

FEBRUARY, 1862.

On and after SATURDAY, FEBRUARY 1st, 1862, the SEVERN VALLEY RAILWAY will be OPENED for Public Traffic, and Trains will run as follows:---

Miles.		1	2	3	4
		P.M.	A.M.	A.M.	A.M.
	Kingstown ...	7 15			7 0
	Holyhead ...	A.M. 2 0	2 0	6 50	11 40
	Liverpool [Landing Stage] ...		7 50	10 50	3 15
	Birkenhead ...		8 10	11 10	3 35
	Manchester ...		6 55	10 5	2 30
	Warrington ...		7 50	10 50	3 15
	Chester ...		8 55	12 0	4 15
		1, 2, & Parl.	1 & 2	1, 2, & 3	1 & 2
	Shrewsbury ...	6 30	10 50	3 0	5 45
4½	Berrington ...	6 42	11 1	3 10	5 57
8½	Cressage ...	6 54	11 12	3 20	6 9
12¾	Buildwas ...	7 6	11 25	3 30	6 21
	Much Wenlock (arr.) ...		11 50	3 55	6 45
	,, (dep. for Up Train)...		11 5	3 10	6 0
13¾	Ironbridge ...	7 14	11 33	3 38	6 29
15¾	Coalport ...	7 20	11 39	3 44	6 35
18	Linley ...	7 31		3 55	
22½	Bridgnorth ...	7 41	11 55	4 3	6 55
27	Hampton ...	7 54	12 5	4 15	
29	Highley ...	8 3	12 13	4 24	
31½	Arley ...	8 12	12 22	4 33	
35	Bewdley ...	8 24	12 33	4 43	
37¾	Stourport ...	8 33	12 43	4 53	
40½	Hartlebury (arr.) ...	8 45	12 53	5 5	
	,, (dep.) ...	9 13	12 58	5 10	
	Kidderminster ...	9 25	1 10	5 30	
	Stourbridge ...	9 33	1 32	5 52	
	Dudley ...	10 17	1 58	6 20	
	Birmingham ...	11 5	2 40	7 5	
	Wolverhampton ...	10 50	2 35	6 50	
51½	Worcester (arr.) ...	9 30	1 35	5 40	
	,, (dep.) ...		1 45	6 25	
	Malvern (arr.) ...	10 35	2 20	6 15	
	Oxford (arr.) ...	12 5	3 50	8 45	
	London [Paddington] ...	2 30	5 40	10 20	
	Cheltenham ...	10 52	4 1	7 28	
	Gloucester ...	11 5	4 16	7 55	
	Bristol ...	12 20	5 35	9 40	

Miles.		1	2	3	4
		A.M.	A.M.	A.M.	P.M.
	Bristol ...			7 55	3 30
	Gloucester ...			8 57	4 34
	Cheltenham ...		6 15	9 28	5 0
	London [Paddington] ...			6 0	1 30
	Oxford ...			8 35	3 25
	Malvern ...			11 0	5 5
	Worcester (arr.) ...			11 0	5 30
	,, (dep.) ...		8 45	11 35	5 45
	Wolverhampton ...	7 30	8 45	10 20	4 30
	Birmingham ...	6 0	8 0	10 20	4 15
	Dudley ...	8 0	9 10	10 55	4 55
	Stourbridge ...	8 25	9 20	11 18	5 15
	Kidderminster ...	8 48	9 33	11 40	5 37
		1, 2, & Parl.	1, 2, & Parl.	1 & 2	1, 2, & 3
11	Hartlebury (arr.) ...	8 55	9 40	11 55	5 45
	,, (dep.) ...		9 50	12 13	6 25
13¾	Stourport ...		10 0	12 23	6 35
16½	Bewdley ...		10 9	12 33	6 44
20	Arley ...		10 21	12 45	6 56
22½	Highley ...		10 30	12 54	7 5
24½	Hampton ...		10 39	1 3	7 14
		1 & 2			
29	Bridgnorth (dep.) ...	9 0	10 50	1 14	7 25
33½	Linley ...	9 10	11 0		7 35
36	Coalport ...	9 21	11 11	1 29	7 46
38	Ironbridge ...	9 27	11 17	1 35	7 52
39½	Buildwas ...	9 35	11 25	1 42	8 0
	Much Wenlock (arr.) ...	10 0	11 50	2 8	8 25
	,, (dep. for Down Train)	9 15	11 5	1 20	7 40
43	Cressage ...	9 47	11 37	1 53	8 12
47	Berrington ...	9 59	11 49	2 4	8 24
51½	Shrewsbury ...	10 10	12 0	2 15	8 35
	Chester ...	11 45	2 5	4 5	10 20
	Warrington ...	12 45	2 53	5 10	
	Manchester ...	1 45	3 40	6 0	
	Birkenhead ...	12 40	2 45	4 50	10 55
	Liverpool ...	1 0	3 5	5 10	11 10
	Holyhead ...	3 5	4 45	9 10	
	Kingstown ...	7 5			

The Times shown in this Table are those before which the Trains will not depart from the various Stations: but the Company cannot guarantee any time, nor will they hold themselves responsible for delay. The Company will not be responsible for the accuracy of the hours of departure and arrival of the Trains of other Companies, as stated in this Table, as they are subject to alterations and delays over which the Company has no control.---SINGLE TICKETS are available ONLY for the Day and Train by which they are issued.

DURING THE MONTH OF FEBRUARY NO SUNDAY TRAINS WILL BE RUN.

A. C. SHERRIFF, General Manager.

PRINTED BY KNIGHT & CO. CHRONICLE OFFICE, 65, BROAD STREET, WORCESTER.

on the Severn. It was twice inspected by Col Yolland for the BoT, at the same times as he inspected the SVR, and his reports are dated 30 December 1861 and 30 January 1862. He was concerned about safety on the steep gradients. On his first inspection he found that runaway vehicles would go onto the SVR and he required weighted safety points to direct them into a blind siding. The turntable at Much Wenlock was not finished and signals were not yet in working order, and so he would not authorise opening. The works were completed in time for his second inspection on 30 January 1862 and he recommended that opening should be sanctioned. It was opened on the same day as the SVR, 1 February.

From the other direction the Shrewsbury & Birmingham had already opened its branch from Madeley Junction to Lightmoor on 1 June 1854. Two months later the Shrewsbury & Birmingham and Shrewsbury & Chester were amalgamated with the GWR.[3] Another company, the Wellington & Severn Junction, incorporated in 1853[4] opened its line from the GWR Shrewsbury & Birmingham line about 2 miles east of Wellington to join the Madeley branch at Lightmoor on 1 May 1857. This railway was worked by the Coalbrookdale Co until 1 July 1861 when it was leased to the GWR and WMR companies.[5] It was finally vested in the GWR from 1 July 1892.[6] (See map, p19)

In 1860 the WMR and SVR companies prepared plans for the Bewdley - Kidderminster loop, to be dealt with later, and a branch from near Benthall Edge, across the Severn and through Coalbrookdale to join the Wellington & Severn Junction Railway near Lightmoor. The engineer, Edward Wilson, was chief engineer of the WMR. The bill went before Parliament in February 1861 but in June the Commons Committee found the preamble relating to the Lightmoor branch not proved and that section of the bill was struck out in favour of a bill presented by the Wenlock Railway Co for the Much Wenlock, Craven Arms & Coalbrookdale Railway. John Fowler, the engineer, prepared plans for a line from Much Wenlock to the Shrewsbury & Hereford Railway at Marsh Farm Junction north of Craven Arms, involving gradients of 1 in 45 and 48 from Much Wenlock up to a summit of 635ft near Presthope on Wenlock Edge. The other portion of the railway left the SVR at Buildwas, crossed the Severn by a bridge identical to the Victoria Bridge and terminated in Coalbrookdale. The Wenlock Railway Act of 22 July 1861 c 189 gave powers to construct the lines and to raise capital of £125,000 and power to borrow £41,500. The major work was the bridge over the Severn, cast and erected by the Coalbrookdale Co using the same patterns as for the Victoria Bridge of two years earlier, but this bridge, named the Albert Edward Bridge after the Prince of Wales, later Edward VII, carried a double line of rails on the two outer pairs of ribs. (The Victoria Bridge was also designed for double track but carried only a single line on the inner pair of ribs.) The Albert Edward Bridge was tested by Capt Tyler in November 1864 and was found to deflect $^{1}/_{2}$in under a load of 400 tons and then to return, which Tyler considered good. The resident engineer was Joseph Fogerty.[7] Today the bridge carries Class 56 diesels on merry-go-round trains of coal for Ironbridge Power Station.

While this railway was being built a GWR Act of 1861[8] authorised a $1^{1}/_{2}$ mile extension from the GWR Madeley branch at Lightmoor to Coalbrookdale where it joined the Wenlock Railway. Both this and the Buildwas - Coalbrookdale line were opened on 1 November 1864. The section from Much Wenlock to Presthope was opened on 5 December 1864, and soon hundreds of tons of limestone were going down the railway each week from the quarries at Westwood and Presthope for the fluxing of iron in the works of the Coalbrookdale Co.[9] The extension to Marsh Farm Junction north of Craven Arms was inspected by Col Rich in September 1867 but he was not satisfied and various further works had to be carried out before the line could be opened on 16 December 1867. Passenger traffic was never of more than local importance, but it was a delightful ride. From where the train emerged from Presthope tunnel (198yd) onto the Wenlock Edge the passenger was afforded wonderful views across Ape Dale to the hills above Church Stretton. The Much Wenlock & Severn Junction and Wenlock Railways were worked by the GWR under an agreement dated 24 March 1864[10] and they were vested in the GWR in 1896.[11]

Over on the other side of the Wyre Forest the Tenbury Railway Co was incorporated in 1859 to construct a railway $4^3/_4$ miles long from the Shrewsbury & Hereford at Woofferton to Tenbury. The company bought part of the Leominster Canal from the Shrewsbury & Hereford Railway, to which it had been sold in 1847, and incorporated three short lengths into the railway formation. The line was opened on 1 August 1861 and was worked by the S&H Co. The proprietors of the Leominster Canal had intended to drive it through to the Severn near Stourport, but heavy tunnelling would have been required; so in 1794 construction was abandoned following collapse of Southnet tunnel, about 5 miles east of Tenbury. Proposals to build a tramway to the Severn never materialised.

While the Tenbury Railway was being built another closely related company, the Tenbury, Bewdley, Kidderminster & Worcester Junction, was projecting an extension through the Wyre Forest to join the SVR at Bewdley. The Tenbury & Bewdley Railway Act of 3 July 1860 c128 incorporated the company with a capital of £120,000 and gave powers for construction of the railway $14^1/_4$ miles long. Further use was made of portions of the Leominster Canal under Section 31 of the Act. The engineers were John Fowler assisted by D. Wylie, and the contract, at a price of £107,000, was awarded to Brassey & Field. The WMR and SVR companies subscribed together £15,000.[12] At the half-yearly meeting of the company at Tenbury on 24 September 1862 it was reported that the foundations for the bridge over the Severn were in hand.[13] It was confidently predicted that the line would be open by 1 January 1864. As on the SVR, however, the work was delayed by severe slips. The railway followed the Teme valley to Newnham Bridge then turned up the Rea valley and along an embankment beside which the Rea was diverted into a new channel, leaving an oxbow lake on the west side of the line. Beyond Neen Sollars it crossed the Rea by a brick arch and passed through undulating country. Just south of Cleobury Mortimer station it curved through a cutting 65ft deep where seams of coal were exposed. A tunnel was intended here but the treacherous nature of the ground made it impracticable, and there was much trouble with slips. A road is carried over the cutting on a lofty three-arched red-brick bridge. This was the summit at 375ft, to which the line climbed at 1 in 80 and 82. From here was a descent with a ruling gradient of 1 in 70 to a level of 85ft at the Dowles bridge carrying the line over the Severn. This consisted of three lattice girder deck spans of 70ft on stone abutments and piers. Beyond the bridge the line curved southwards and climbed up alongside the SVR which it paralleled to the junction at the north end of Bewdley station.

On 5 August 1864 the first passenger train passed over the line as a pleasure trip for the directors and their friends. On 9 August the line was inspected for the BoT. The train standing on the Dowles bridge in the photograph on p68 is believed to be the inspector's train. It is headed by the then brand new Wolverhampton-built 2–4–0 well tank No 1A which was renumbered 17 in July 1865. Public traffic began on 13 August.[14] Right to the end the branch was operated in two portions with a change at Tenbury. It was worked by the GWR under an agreement dated 29 July 1863 between the WMR, SVR and Tenbury & Bewdley companies. The Shrewsbury & Hereford, which had been operating the Tenbury Railway, between Woofferton and Tenbury, was leased to the LNWR, GWR and WMR companies from 1 July 1862,[15] and the Tenbury Railway was transferred to the LNWR and GWR companies jointly by indenture dated 1 December 1868.[16] The Tenbury & Bewdley Railway was vested in the GWR by the GWR Act of 12 July 1869 c109.

This railway was seen as a through route between districts beyond the Shrewsbury & Hereford and the industrial towns of the West Midlands, in which the LNWR was keenly interested. To reach it from these parts involved an inconvenient reversal at Hartlebury. Clearly a direct connection from

Bewdley to Kidderminster would be necessary to enable the line to Woofferton to fulfil its function as a through route. As yet Kidderminster had no rail connection with Birmingham except via Dudley, but the Stourbridge Railway and extension were under construction. To people in the Severn valley from Bewdley to Bridgnorth the proposed line would form a convenient route to Kidderminster and beyond.

The loop was laid out in 1860 by Edward Wilson, engineer of what was still the OWW at Worcester. His plan showed the line leaving the SVR at the south end of the Sandbourne viaduct, at a height of 125ft above OD, passing through a tunnel 400yd long, 91ft 6in below ground, crossing the Staffordshire & Worcestershire Canal and the River Stour by a viaduct and joining the OWW south of Kidderminster station at a height of 197ft. The total length was 2 miles 76 chains.

The West Midland & Severn Valley Companies Act of 1 August 1861 c 212 authorised construction of the line from a junction with the SVR 'at or near the Southern End of the Sambourn (sic) Viaduct thereof' to a junction with the WMR (by which title the OWW was then known) 'at a point about two furlongs south of the Booking Office at Kidderminster Station.' Section 9 ruled that the bridge over the Staffordshire & Worcestershire Canal was to be 30ft between abutments and 20ft clear above water. The railway was to form part of the SVR, and four years were allowed for completion. Powers were granted to the SVR to raise £60,000 additional capital and to borrow up to £20,000 on mortgage. It must be remembered that the SVR was still under construction at the time of this Act, and with problems arising from landslips the company had enough troubles for the time being. Also completion of the Tenbury line was still three years ahead, so further progress on the loop to Kidderminster was delayed. Meanwhile responsibility for the 1861 Act passed to the GWR and it was discussed at a board meeting on 1 October 1863. Edward Wilson was instructed to prepare a plan and section and to submit an estimate, although he had done this already for the 1861 Bill.

The LNWR company's interest in the Bewdley - Kidderminster loop was shown in an agreement, dated 17 March 1863, between the LNWR and the GWR/WMR. By it the GWR sought to forestall LNWR opposition to its absorption of the WMR later that year, and it also gained access to Manchester. In return the GWR granted running powers to the LNWR between Smethwick and Stourbridge and Bewdley. The GWR and WMR were to complete the Bewdley

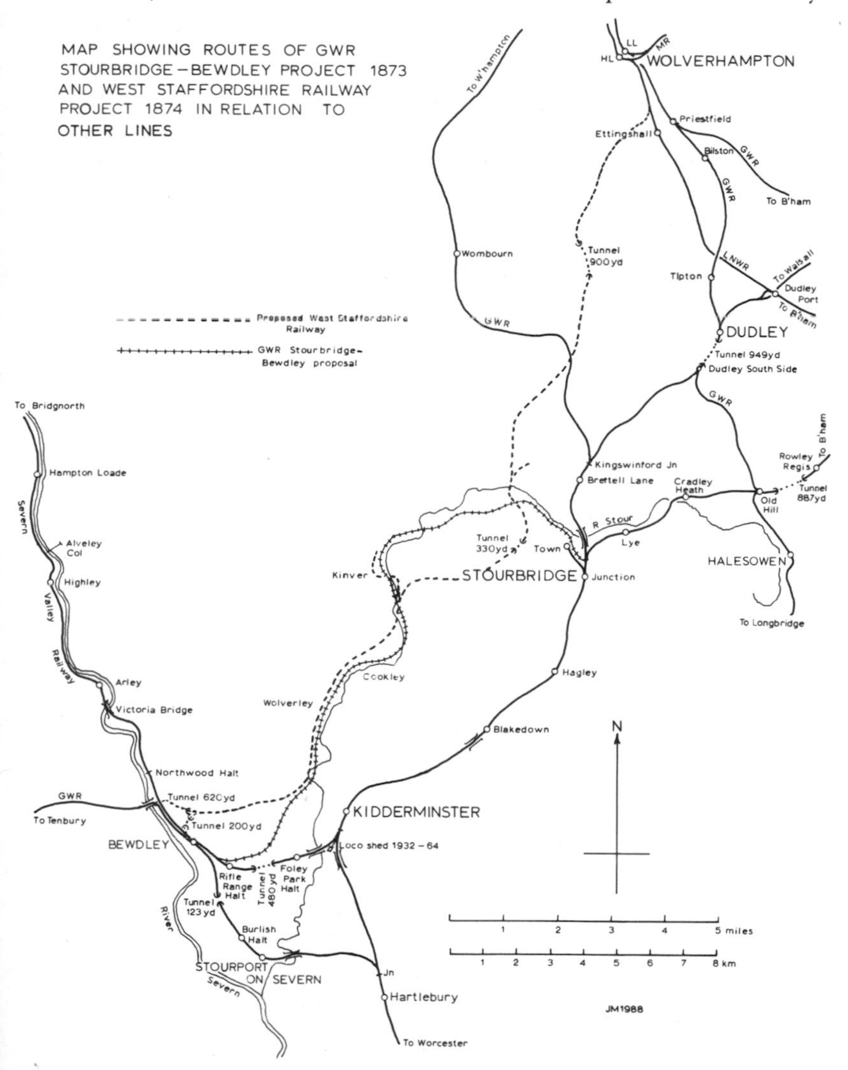

- Kidderminster loop on or before 1 July 1865. At that time the LNWR line from Abergavenny to Merthyr, begun in 1860, was still far from completion. It was opened to Brynmawr on 29 September 1862, Nantybwch on 1 March 1864, Rhymney on 5 September 1871, but it was 1 June 1879 before trains could reach Merthyr through the Morlais tunnel. In view of this the LNWR was hardly in a position from which it could enforce the terms relating to completion of the loop.

In a letter dated 29 September 1863 Wilson stated that the cost of a single line between Kidderminster and Bewdley with a double junction at Kidderminster and single junction at Bewdley would be £57,000, and that he was preparing (another ?) plan and section. On 21 January 1864 the board adopted a recommendation to proceed with the loop, and on 28 April was advised that powers for purchasing land for it would shortly expire and the deposit of £4,800 would be forfeited if the railway was not built. Wilson recommended that a double line should be constructed although the Act provided for only a single line. The directors authorised construction of a double line 'under the circumstances stated', whatever that meant. At a meeting on 21 July the following ten directors were requested to sign a subscription contract on behalf of the GWR Co, each to the extent of £6,000: Captain Thomas Bulkeley, C.R.M. Talbot, Edward Greaves, Edward Leeming, John Williams, Richard Mitchell, Richard Bussett, John William Miles, Charles A. Wood, and L.L. Dillwyn. The board undertook to indemnify each director from any liability arising therefrom. In a letter dated 24 November 1864, read at a board meeting on 8 December, Edward Wilson presented an estimate of £55,133. The board considered that construction of the line should go ahead without delay and the chairman was authorised to do whatever was necessary for this.[18] At a special meeting of the SVR shareholders on 14 December it was resolved that in accordance with arrangements with the GWR Co and to enable the SVR Co to construct the loop, the directors should be authorised to create and issue the new share capital of £60,000 and, as soon as they legally could, the debentures of £20,000 authorised in the WMR and SVR companies' Act of 1861, and to attach to the capital an interest of $4^1/_2$ per cent per annum.

Another important influence on the course of events concerning the Kidderminster loop was the Stourbridge Railway Co, closely associated with the OWW. In 1860 it obtained powers to construct a railway from the OWW at Stourbridge station to Old Hill, and in 1861 for the Stourbridge Extension Railway from Old Hill to join the LNWR Birmingham - Wolverhampton line at Smethwick. By the GWR Act of 1862 another connection was authorised from Smethwick to the Birmingham, Wolverhampton & Dudley line of the GWR at Handsworth. The line was opened from Stourbridge to Cradley on 1 April 1863, but difficulties with Old Hill tunnel delayed the opening to Smethwick, Handsworth and Galton junctions until 1 April 1867. Meanwhile the Stourbridge Co obtained powers in 1865 for a branch to Stourbridge town centre, leaving the OWW by a north-facing junction and curving round through almost half a circle. Later that year plans were prepared for the company by Edward Wilson for the 'Valley of the Stour Extension', including a deviation of the authorised Stourbridge Town branch, and continuing it by a line running northwards then westwards along the Stour valley and following this via Kinver and Wolverley. Here it was to leave the Stour and pass 2 miles north of Kidderminster to join the SVR by a north-facing junction north of Bewdley station (see map p59). Clearly this was intended to feed traffic to and from the Tenbury line onto the Stourbridge Railway. Only the deviation of the Stourbridge branch managed to get through to the Stourbridge Railway Act of 1866. The Valley of the Stour Extension was thrown out of the bill. Its failure to serve either Kidderminster or Bewdley went against it, and there was opposition from the LNWR and the Staffordshire & Worcestershire Canal Co, but the scheme for a railway from Stourbridge through Kinver and Wolverley to Kidderminster and Bewdley was to reappear later.

In the early 1860s the GWR, in common with other

British railway companies, was entering a period of financial restraint which lasted until 1869, and the company regarded the Bewdley - Kidderminster loop as an unnecessary expense. But the matter was kept alive and in 1867 a new plan and section was prepared by Michael Lane, the GWR chief civil engineer. It was almost his last work for the company for he died in London on 27 February 1868 at the age of 65. His route was roughly the same as Wilson's; gradients were slightly different, the tunnel was to be 484yd long, the rails 89ft below ground; a viaduct 44yd long, carried the line 58ft 9in above the canal and 66ft above the Stour. The Worcester road was to be crossed by an arch of 35ft span 16ft high, carrying the rails 38ft 6in above the road.

The preamble to the bill of 1868 stated that the purpose was 'to extend the time and to revive the powers' of the 1861 Act, which powers had expired in 1865. The GWR Act of 31 July 1868 c 145 revived powers for the loop and gave five years to complete the work with a penalty of £50 per day if not completed. Money deposited under the WMR & SVR Act of 1861 was made applicable to this Act. Under Section 23 of the 1861 Act £4,800, or 8 per cent on £60,000, the estimated cost of the railway, had been deposited in the Court of Chancery. This money was now to be invested in the construction of the loop. Powers were to end after the five years allowed by the Act.

Meanwhile, at the GWR board meeting on 19 October 1871 Mr Grierson, the general manager, reported that, following a request, he had had an interview with the mayor of Kidderminster and principal manufacturers when it was suggested that to provide better railway facilities at Kidderminster the Bewdley - Kidderminster loop should be diverted to pass through the town or, if that were not practicable, then the Stourbridge Railway 'Valley of the Stour Extension' should be altered to serve Kidderminster and that the Bewdley - Kidderminster loop should be abandoned. Mr Grierson was asked to go over the route, which he did, presumably on foot through some rough muddy country, and he reported on the route at the following meeting on 2 November. Edward Wilson attended with plans and trial sections he had prepared and it was agreed, subject to the assent of the LNWR Co, to apply to abandon the Bewdley - Kidderminster loop and to obtain powers to construct the Stourbridge - Bewdley line. The matter was brought before the LNWR & GWR Joint Committee and the LNWR assented to the postponement of the Bewdley - Kidderminster loop and that application for the Stourbridge - Bewdley line should stand over for another year to allow time for plans and estimates to be prepared and for the whole question to be considered. It was therefore decided to apply for an extension of the existing powers which was granted for a further three years by the GWR Act of 18 July 1872 c129.

The plan and section for the Stourbridge - Bewdley line, prepared in 1872 by W.G. Owen and Edward Wilson for the 1873 session, showed a line 12 miles 68 chains long from the end of the Stourbridge Railway town branch, authorised in 1866 but still not built, closely following the route of the 'Valley of the Stour Extension' via Kinver, Cookley and Wolverley to the west of Kidderminster, up at 1 in 100 to a cutting 71ft deep through the high ground between there and Bewdley, then down at 1 in 100, skirting the north side of the 'Devil's Spittleful', to join the SVR at the south end of the Sandbourne viaduct. The cost was estimated at £211,000. The bill was examined by the House of Commons Committee in June 1873 and various witnesses gave evidence for and against the line. The chief opponents were the LNWR Co which argued that it had strong interests in the Bewdley loop line, and the proprietors of the Staffordshire & Worcestershire Canal who saw the line as a threat to their traffic. On 12 June the committee declared the preamble of the bill was not proved and the line was struck off, and the GWR was ordered to proceed at once with the Bewdley loop.[19] Compared with the loop the Stourbridge - Bewdley project looked ridiculous, with nearly 8 miles up or down at 1 in 100, and a total distance from Stourbridge Junction to Bewdley 3 miles longer than via the loop. Its only justification was that it would serve a few industries in the Stour valley, already served by the canal.

The following day, 13 June, Daniel Gooch, the GWR chairman, addressed a special general meeting called to discuss the bill. Referring to the Stourbridge - Bewdley project he remarked: 'That portion of the bill is thrown out and you will now be obliged to proceed with your Kidderminster curve, and finish the obligation you took upon yourselves I don't know how long ago - some ten or twelve years ago - and which you have been putting off until the present time.'[20] Poor Gooch was feeling dejected; five days earlier he had had to leave Brunel's *Great Eastern* steamship off the Isle of Wight and watch it sail away without him to lay the second Atlantic cable.[21] He would dearly have loved to go again, as he had when the first cable was laid. Addressing the half-yearly meeting of GWR shareholders on 27 August 1873 Gooch regretted the decision of the parliamentary committee and spoke of the Bewdley loop as a 'useless curve' which they did not want and were now compelled to build, and which would probably cost much more than the £60,000 in the original 1861 Act.[22]

On 3 December 1873 the agent, Mr Bull, agreed to carry out the purchase of land for the loop on terms proposed in 1865 as follows: Earl of Dudley, 3 acres, £3,300 including compensation for abolishing the level crossing at the point of junction at Kidderminster (It was replaced by the long footbridge, still in use.); the vicar of Kidderminster, 12 acres, £2,500; W.C. Hemming, 7 acres, £1,657; and S. Baker, 5 acres, £1,050; total £8,507. The Staffordshire & Worcestershire Canal Co consented to an alteration in the viaduct over the canal, on payment of £125 which included the cost of land and the right of a perpetual easement (right of way) over the canal.

Although something seemed to be moving at last, the GWR Co was in no hurry to start work on the loop. What finally spurred the company into action was the appearance of a new project, strongly backed by the LNWR, under the title of the West Staffordshire Railway, for a line from Wolverhampton to join the Tenbury line at Bewdley. The bill, prepared in 1874, was opposed by the GWR and canal companies but it received strong support from various manufacturers and local

Stourport station about 1900 (K. Beddoes/W. Smith Collection)

Two GWR diesel railcars in Stourport station on 24 August 1959; left the 16.58 Tenbury – Hartlebury; right 17.30 Hartlebury – Bewdley (John Marshall)

North end of Mount Pleasant tunnel, 1968 (Martin Wynne)

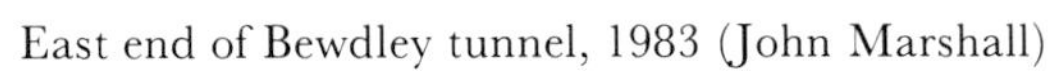

East end of Bewdley tunnel, 1983 (John Marshall)

Leaving Bewdley for Kidderminster on the Sandbourne viaduct, 6 September 1963. Original SVR line to Hartlebury on right. Bewdley by-pass bridge is now just beyond the viaduct. (Peter E. Baughan)

Bewdley station from south end of island platform with 2–4–0 'Metro' tank on train to Hartlebury

Wolverhampton 2–4–0 well tank No 1A, as built in 1864, on Dowles Bridge on the Tenbury line with the inspector's train on 9 August 1864. The engine was renumbered 17 in July 1865. The barge on the right was used by the contractor, Thomas Brassey (BR/OPC)

GWR 2–4–0 No 180 on Bewdley viaduct in 1897. The engine was built in 1853 (R & W Hawthorn 829) and became OWW No 16, and GWR No 180 in 1863. Withdrawn 1899. (Bewdley Museum)

'Beyer Goods' 0–6–0 No 334 approaching Bewdley from Shrewsbury in the early 1900s. The footbridge, erected in 1892, was removed in the 1930s. (K. Beddoes/W. Smith Collection)

6960 *Raveningham Hall* crossing Victoria Bridge, 10 April 1988 (John Marshall)

Arley station, one of the 'best preserved stations', 10 April 1988 (John Marshall)

Ivatt 2–6–0 No 46521 crossing Borle viaduct, going south, on 19 September 1982. The view shows the ten tie bars inserted when the viaduct was repaired in 1976–7. (John Marshall)

The 16.20 Shrewsbury – Hartlebury railcar at Highley on 6 September 1963. The view, looking south, shows the footbridge built in 1914 and removed by the SVR in 1974. (Peter E. Baughan)

Alveley Halt, looking north, 6 September 1963. Built in 1939 to serve the colliery. (Peter E. Baughan)

Alveley Sidings and coal screens looking north, 6 September 1963 (Peter E. Baughan)

Hampton Loade station and the original signal box, looking north, 6 September 1963 (Peter E. Baughan)

Eardington Halt, looking north, 6 September 1963 (Peter E. Baughan)

Bridgnorth station from Panpudding Hill, showing the footbridge over Hollybush Road (from an old postcard)

Clarkson 'Chelmsford' steam bus, GWR fleet No 36, outside Wolverhampton Low Level station from where it left for Bridgnorth, 1904–5 (K. Beddoes Collection)

The 16.20 diesel railcar ex Shrewsbury to Hartlebury crossing the steam-hauled 16.10 ex Hartlebury to Shrewsbury at Bridgnorth, 6 September 1963 (Peter E. Baughan)

Bridgnorth tunnel from Shrewsbury train, 8 August 1959 (John Marshall)

Linley Halt, looking north, 6 September 1963 (Peter E. Baughan)

Coalport station, looking south, 6 September 1963 (Peter E. Baughan)

The second Jackfield Halt, opened 1 March 1954, to replace that of 1934 destroyed in the 1952 landslip, looking north on 6 September 1963 (Peter E. Baughan)

Iron Bridge & Broseley station from across the Severn, from a postcard of about 1930 (Peter E. Baughan)

Buildwas Junction SVR platform. Much Wenlock branch platform on right, looking east, 6 September 1963 (Peter E. Baughan)

Cressage station and signal box, looking east, 6 September 1963 (Peter E. Baughan)

The 16.20 railcar ex Shrewsbury to Hartlebury at Cound Halt, 6 September 1963 (Peter E. Baughan)

Berrington station, looking north, 6 September 1963 (Peter E. Baughan).

Former Burnt Mill Junction, Shrewsbury, looking north past the abutments of the Shropshire & Montgomeryshire Railway bridge on 6 September 1963. The cabin housing the auxilliary token instrument is the base of the old Burnt Mill Junction signal box, closed in 1937. (Peter E. Baughan)

Scene at Bridgnorth on 15 October 1967 on one of the early SVR open days, with Ivatt 2–6–0 No 46443 in steam (T. A. Fletcher)

0–6–0 No 3205 in steam at Bridgnorth 15 October 1967 (T. A. Fletcher)

authorities including Bewdley Town Council which openly expressed its impatience with the GWR's dilatoriness in starting work on the loop.

The line, laid out by William Henry Thomas, was to leave the LNWR 'Stour Valley' line about a mile south of Wolverhampton High Level station, to run southwards via Kingswinford, the west side of Stourbridge, Wolverley, and the west side of Kidderminster, then through tunnels 400 and 620yd long, emerging under the SVR to join the Tenbury & Bewdley Railway near the east abutment of the bridge over the Severn. A branch of 57 chains was to pass through a 200yd tunnel to join the SVR at the north end of Bewdley viaduct in Wribbenhall. The length of the main line would be 19 miles 10 chains, the ruling gradient was 1 in 80 and there was a good deal of 1 in 100. The estimated cost of the double-track line with six short branches was £734,525. This was a much superior route to the 1873 GWR project, despite the heavy gradients. The WSR bill had its second reading in the Commons on 14 February 1875. At the examination of the bill by the Commons Committee in March representatives from various local communities and industrialists put forward a strong case for the proposed railway, but in the end the opposition won. It was decided on 18 March that the preamble was not proved and the bill was thrown out. The decision by the GWR to proceed with the Bewdley - Kidderminster loop certainly influenced the failure of the bill.[23]

As soon as the WSR project appeared the GWR applied for a further extension of time for construction of the loop, and by the Act of 1875[24] it was granted another two years. Section 23 of the 1861 Act was now to read as if the period for construction was until 18 July 1877. The tender of Charles Dickinson, £39,800, was accepted on 7 October 1874 and the contract was sealed on 3 December. Despite favourable reports on Dickinson, progress was not satisfactory and Wilson reported on 30 March 1875 that unless there was an improvement special attention would be called to it in the next report. On 31 May Dickinson wrote to the GWR board explaining his difficulty in obtaining stone for the piers of the viaduct and he asked to be allowed the difference in price for brick. This was granted and so the viaduct was built entirely in brick. Work continued through 1875 and 1876. In his report in March 1877 Wilson stated that the tunnel, viaduct and bridges were nearly completed. Delay with the cutting east of the tunnel had been caused by bad weather.[25] This was Wilson's last report on the work; he died at Westminster on 26 August 1877. The resident engineer, Mr Tyrell, continued to direct the work.

At the GWR board meeting on 24 October the general manager submitted a report from W.G. Owen, the GWR chief engineer, on the state of the works on the loop, stating that the junctions, signalling and locking arrangements could be completed in about seven weeks. A plan was submitted of the necessary signalling and locking including the erection of two signal boxes at Bewdley. The expenditure of £1,630 was approved. A letter from George Findlay, then chief traffic manager of the LNWR, was read enquiring if arrangements could be made for a service of goods trains to begin on 1 December and complaining of the delay in completion of the line. But his company had to wait six months longer. On 10 December a plan was submitted of the proposed junction and extension of platforms and other works at Bewdley, estimated to cost £1,655 10s 6d. The plan was approved and Owen was instructed to carry out the works, which were not included in Dickinson's contract.

Bewdley Town Council was becoming impatient with the delay, and on 18 December 1877 the town clerk wrote to James Grierson, the GWR secretary, with a resolution from the council. He received an evasive reply which caused anger at the next council meeting on 14 January 1878. The town clerk explained that there was a good deal of work to be done at Tenbury, before the loop could be opened, to facilitate transfer of LNWR goods traffic, and that the GWR was in the hands of the contractors.

With the line now nearing completion, Dickinson applied to

the GWR on 6 February 1878 to be relieved of maintenance of the works for the first year after opening. The board authorised Owen to arrange with Dickinson for maintenance by the GWR, out of the retention fund, of the bridges and embankments at the actual cost, and for maintenance of permanent way for the first year out of capital.

At last, in March 1878, the loop was completed and on 22 March Colonel Rich, inspector for the BoT, came to examine the line. The inspection train left Kidderminster at about 10.30, carrying Col Rich and a number of officials including H.Y. Adye, traffic superintendent; J. Ward Armstrong, engineer at Hereford; Mr Rowbotham, engineer Wolverhampton; George Armstrong, GWR locomotive superintendent, Wolverhampton; and Charles Dickinson, the contractor. Col Rich pronounced the bridges and viaduct the most satisfactory structures he had ever seen; they were a credit to Mr Dickinson. He was surprised and much amused to find the tunnel lit by candles and naphtha lamps. After minutely inspecting every portion of it he expressed his satisfaction. At Bewdley the layout needed altering to do away with all unnecessary facing points. The turntable at Bewdley was being removed to Woofferton. The lines from Tenbury and Shrewsbury at the west end of the station were to be connected to form a double track through the station, and the same was to be done with the lines from Stourport and Kidderminster at the east end. The loop line round the north of the new island platform was to make a double junction with the through lines at each end of the station. He required a footbridge to be built between the up and down platforms because passengers were having to cross the rails. Also a shelter was to be built on the island platform.

Permanent way consisted of double-headed steel rails 80 lb/yd with inside wooden keys in cast-iron chairs weighing 36 lb each. The track was ballasted with sand and gravel. Much work remained to be done on the signalling. Because of the incomplete state of the works Col Rich refused permission for opening.[27]

This final delay in the opening must have been exasperating, for it was not until 29 May that a second inspection could be made. This time Col Rich gave permission for the line to be opened. The local newspapers carried an advertisement announcing opening on 1 June. Additional trains would be run between Kidderminster, Bewdley and Wooferton (sic) and the service to and from Birmingham and the Bewdley, Tenbury, Wooferton, Leominster and Ludlow districts would be improved. On 1 June 1878 the first public train left Bewdley without ceremony soon after 8.00 and at Kidderminster connected with the 8.25 to Birmingham and Wolverhampton. The first-class fare to Kidderminster was 5d and the 'Parliamentary' fare $3^1/_2$d, considerd to be 'on the high scale for which the Great Western Railway Company are rather notorious.'[28]

CHAPTER 6

Along the Railway

In this chapter the features of the SVR are examined from Hartlebury to Shrewsbury. Developments at each place are dealt with in order of occurrence from the 1860s to the late 1980s, regardless of ownership, be it the West Midland, GWR, BR or the current SVR. It should be borne in mind that the SVR had been leased to the WMR Co before the railway was opened. References in this chapter to the SVR Co relate to the current ownership of the line from Kidderminster to Bewdley and Bridgnorth. Signalling developments and operation are covered in chapter 8.

As shown in Col Yolland's report of his inspection on 30 December 1861[1] the track was laid with double-headed iron rails 71 lb/yd in lengths of 21ft and 24ft fixed by pressure-creosoted pitch pine keys in cast-iron chairs weighing 23 lb each secured to sleepers of 'Memel Riga fir' 8ft 6in x 9in x $4^1/_2$in, spaced at 3ft $2^1/_2$in centres. There were forty-two underbridges, twenty-one overbridges and sixteen viaducts. Of the underbridges four had wrought-iron girders, fifteen cast-iron girders and two were timber. The remainder were of brick or brick and stone. The largest span (excluding Victoria Bridge) was a wrought-iron girder bridge 35ft on the square and 55ft on the skew over the Cleobury Road at Bridgnorth. Of the overbridges three had cast-iron girders, one wrought-iron girders and one was timber. Remaining overbridges were entirely of brick or brick and stone. The greatest span was a segmental arch of 54ft, between Hartlebury and Stourport.

Notes to this chapter are on p 216.

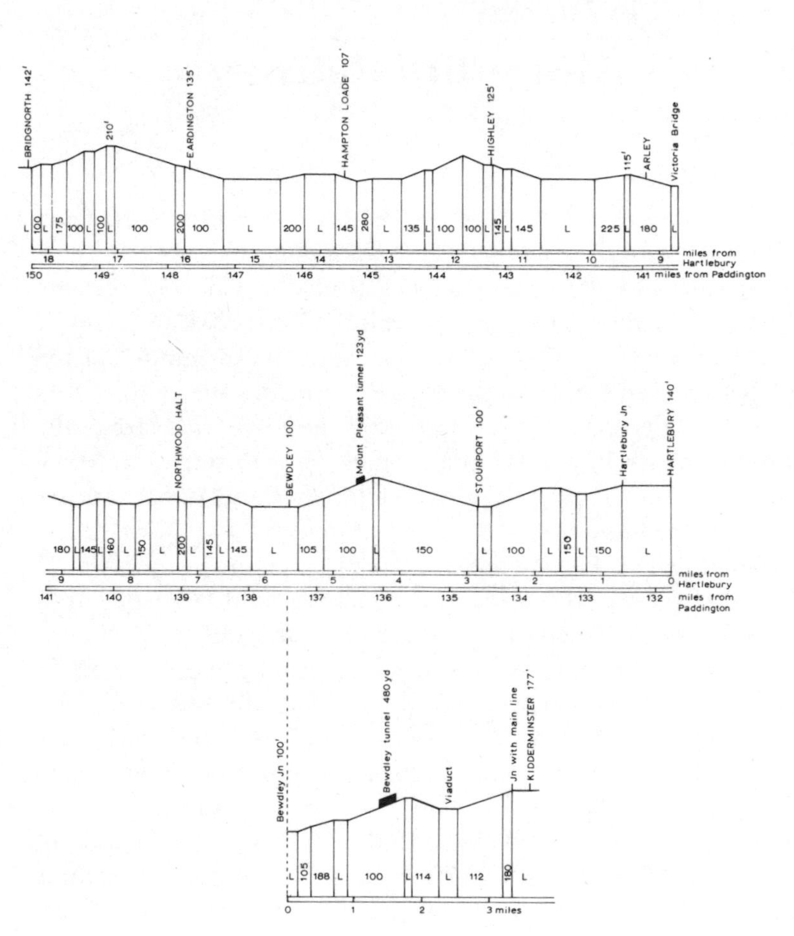
GRADIENTS. BRIDGNORTH TO HARTLEBURY AND KIDDERMINSTER
BRIDGNORTH 142'
210'
EARDINGTON 135'
HAMPTON LOADE 107'
HIGHLEY 125'
115'
ARLEY
Victoria Bridge
miles from Hartlebury
miles from Paddington
NORTHWOOD HALT
BEWDLEY 100
Mount Pleasant tunnel 123yd
STOURPORT 100'
Hartlebury Jn
HARTLEBURY 140'
Bewdley Jn 100'
Bewdley tunnel 480yd
Viaduct
Jn with main line
KIDDERMINSTER 177'
3 miles

At the opening of the OWW north of Droitwich on 3 May 1852 Hartlebury was a small wayside station with a simple wooden shed. With the opening of the SVR ten years later it became a junction station and more accommodation was needed. The construction of a new station at a cost of £300 was authorised on 6 April 1865. The junction was about 600yd north of the station. A through plate girder span carried the line over the Kidderminster - Worcester road, now A449. The bridge was demolished in 1985.

About $1^1/_4$ miles from Hartlebury, at 133 miles 53ch, the Regent Oil Co opened a depot on 28 August 1939, just before the outbreak of war. It was known as Leapgate Private Sidings and the connection trailed in on the left. The name derives from the 'Leap Gate' of the ancient deer park adjoining Hartlebury Common. There were two sidings, one on each side of a gantry, and each would accommodate thirteen 20-ton to seventeen 10-ton tank wagons. The depot had no road connection. Access was controlled by a two-lever ground frame operating points and facing point lock (FPL), released by the electric token for the Hartlebury - Stourport section. Up to thirty wagons, with brake van leading, could be propelled from Stourport to the sidings.

Beyond here the line entered the cutting where excavation was described in chapter 4, a third of a mile long, 60ft deep, spanned by a lofty brick arch 54ft span sprung from the sandstone each side. A large sand quarry on the right was served by a siding which trailed in about $^3/_4$ mile south of Stourport signal box. The points were worked by a ground frame locked by the section token. After the quarry closed, the siding was used to store trains of coal waiting for entry to Stourport power station.

Immediately beyond the cutting the line crossed Wilden Lane by a skew segmental arch 24ft span on the square. An embankment led to the viaduct across the River Stour which was crossed by a skew segmental arch 42ft span on the square and 51ft on the skew. One semicircular arch 24ft span to the east and three to the west of the river completed the viaduct which was built of massive sandstone blocks with arches turned in brick. The embankment continued for 500yd to a brick viaduct over Timber Lane of three semicircular arches 24ft 6in span.

The construction of a power station by the River Severn at Stourport was authorised in 1918, together with a branch railway 7.3f long from the SVR 25yd east of the bridge over the Staffordshire & Worcestershire Canal.[2] The power station was built but not the railway, and the powers for this lapsed. They were renewed in 1938;[3] the railway was built and was brought into use early in 1940. From a junction facing west the single-line branch turned southwards, crossed Mill Road, the River Stour and Hartlebury Road on plate girder bridges. At about $^3/_4$ mile it fanned out into a nest of eight sidings. The branch continued over Worcester Road on another plate girder bridge (dismantled on 4 February 1986) and entered the power station precincts. For shunting in the sidings the electricity authority had two 0–4–0 saddle tanks by Barclay and Peckett.[4] 'Main line' locomotives were not allowed beyond the Worcester Road bridge. BR continued to work coal to the power station until March 1979. The track from Hartlebury Junction to Stourport Power Station was finally lifted during 1983. A footpath passes beneath the junction in a long tunnel. A segmental skew brick arch 33ft span carried the line over the Staffordshire & Worcestershire Canal.

Stourport, $2^3/_4$ miles, was one of the principal stations on

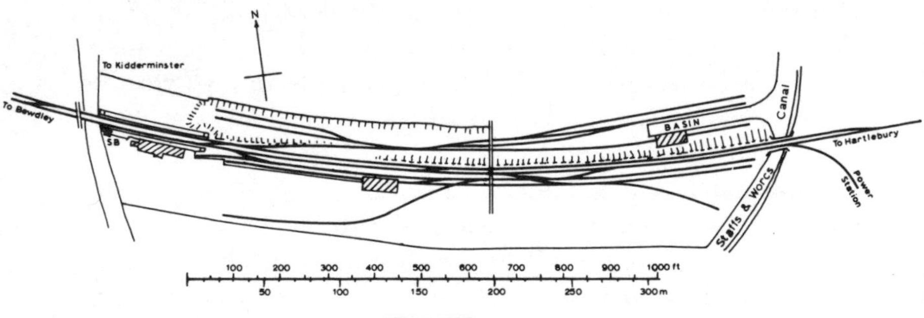

STOURPORT

the SVR. It was renamed Stourport-on-Severn in October 1934, perhaps to avoid confusion with Stourbridge, for there was no other Stourport station. At Wilden, about a mile up the Stour, an ironworks was established in the 17th century. In 1840 it was taken over by the Baldwin family. It was connected to the S&W canal by the river and a short link canal. Under Alfred Baldwin[5] in the 1880s it flourished, and so that it could make use of the railway for deliveries of iron and coal, an interchange basin was constructed by the GWR beside the line at Stourport. Why a short branch railway was not constructed is not clear. The first mention of the basin was in the GWR board minutes on 5 March 1884 when its construction was authorised at an estimated total cost of £4,771. In a letter to the canal company dated 1 May J. Ward Armstrong, divisional engineer at Hereford, stated that the GWR Co intended making a dock about 300ft x 24ft and asked about thickness of puddle. W. Jones of the canal company recommended 12in.[6] On 30 July the tender of S.C. Frayne, £1,516, was accepted for construction of the basin and goods warehouse. It must have been finished about the end of February 1885 for on 2 March the secretary of the canal company read a letter asking that the water might be drawn off so that the new basin could be connected to the canal. The rail connection to the basin made a facing junction with the up line just east of the station and dropped down steeply to three sidings, one on the south where there was a goods shed, and two on the north side of the basin. To this basin the GWR brought iron and later steel from South Wales and coal from Highley colliery, to be taken by canal and river to Wilden ironworks. More sidings, below the station, at a cost of £1,273, were approved on 8 August 1906. A one-ton crane was installed at the basin, at a cost of £80, in 1912. Instructions for working the sidings at the basin still appeared in the sectional appendix to the working timetable printed in October 1960, although by then there could have been hardly any canal traffic.

In 1889 the GWR sought to close a footway crossing just east of Stourport station, but in response to a petition from the Kidderminster Highways Board it was decided to erect a footbridge. The expenditure of £600 for this, authorised on 9 October 1890, seems excessive. At the west end of the station the railway crossed the Kidderminster road on the level. In 1896 the Kidderminster & Stourport Electric Tramway Act authorised the construction of one of Britain's earliest electric tramways. As it was to cross the railway on the level, the opportunity was taken to extend the passing loop beyond the level crossing, at a cost of £349 of which £202 was reimbursed by the tramway company.

The level crossing of the 3ft 6in gauge tramway and two lines of railway track at a skew angle presented unusual problems, and the GWR drawing[7] dated 27 March 1897 carries pencil notes and sketches showing how it had to be modified to get it to fit together. The tramway, opened on 23 May 1898,[8] provided a direct journey to Kidderminster and its effect on the railway is described in Chapter 8. It was closed on 2 April 1929.

Further siding accommodation west of the level crossing was authorised on 11 April 1913 at a cost of £3,222 plus £700 for land and this was included in the GWR Act of 1914.[9] Beyond here Burlish Halt, 3¼ miles, had one platform on the right. It was opened on 31 March 1930.[10] Sidings on the left, with a junction facing Stourport, served the works of Steatite & Porcelain Products Ltd opened in 1929. At first there was a connection to the works crossing the Stourport - Bewdley road. This was closed in 1933 but the sidings remained in use beside the SVR. Further on, at Burlish Crossing, the crossing keeper's house on the left beyond the crossing is now a private dwelling.

A deep cutting through sandstone led to Mount Pleasant tunnel, straight, 124yd long, with moulded stone archivolts at each end. It was 16ft wide at rail level and 16ft high, with a brick arch throughout and brick-lined walls except for about 40 yards at the north end. The excessively wide cutting at the north end appears to have served as a borrow pit for the embankment beyond, pierced by two stone-arch under bridges, the first of massive construction 30ft span and 28ft high. The loop from Kidderminster comes in on the right and the line crosses Bewdley by-pass on a concrete bridge 60ft span on the skew, 44ft on the square.

Unlike Bridgnorth by-pass, of which details are given in chapter 9 p189, this was built at no cost to the SVR. The bridge was built on a concrete track on the south side of the embankment. Work began in May 1986 and the bridge was completed in October. Immediately after the last train had passed on Sunday 19 October track was removed by SVR volunteers and signal wires etc disconnected. At 01.00 on Monday 20th in went the excavators and by next morning there was a great gap in the embankment. By the beginning of November the concrete tracks, foundation and north wing walls were completed and at 07.30 on 6 November the great move began. Two powerful hydraulic rams working on high tensile threaded steel rods pushed the 2,500 ton concrete bridge about 150ft into its final position where it arrived with perfect precision at 10.40. The south wing walls were soon constructed and the embankment was replaced, every foot or so thoroughly consolidated. On 26 November ballast was spread over the bridge and the track relaid, and the first trains crossed on Saturday, 29 November. The entire work was a credit to the contractor, A. Monk & Co Ltd, and the SVR permanent way gang. The by-pass was opened on 21 May 1987 (pp153–4).

Sandbourne viaduct, 101yd long, double track width, has ten arches of 25ft span turned in brick, and sandstone piers and spandrels. The provision of a railing along the coping of both walls of the viaduct, at a cost of £27, was approved on 27 November 1893. The junction between the two lines was at Bewdley South Box, in a sandstone cutting.

At this point we can digress to look at the Kidderminster loop. South of Kidderminster station it veers off to the right. On the left just beyond the Hoo Road overbridge was the 'new' Kidderminster locomotive depot, opened in 1932 to replace the original small shed near the station, and closed in 1964 (see chapter 8 p137). The site is now covered by houses. Worcester Road is crossed by a brick arch of 30ft span. Falling Sands viaduct, in red brick, of seven semicircular arches of 46ft span, 132yd long and 25ft between parapets, carries the line over the River Stour and the S&W canal. On the left beyond here sidings were laid in 1925 to serve the sugar factory and were used until 1980. Foley Park Halt was opened on 2 January 1905 (see chapter 8 p143). Originally it was on the south side of the line but was moved to the north side when the sugar sidings were installed. It remained in use until the line was closed to passengers on 6 January 1970. It has not been reopened. It was connected by a path to the Stourport Road which is carried over the line here on a segmental brick arch.

A sandstone cutting leads to Bewdley tunnel, 480yd long and originally 19ft wide. Despite Col Rich's satisfaction with the tunnel in 1878, on 13 March 1888, barely ten years later, Mr Rowbotham, divisional engineer, Wolverhampton, reported that a portion of the arch was giving way. Emergency repairs were undertaken to safeguard the traffic, and from time to time afterwards various lengths of the tunnel were repaired, amounting in all to about 4½ chains. In 1908 it was found that the whole tunnel lining was deteriorating, so on 23 October the board authorised an expenditure of £700 on repairs to the arch. As this proceeded further, repairs in the roof and sidewalls were found to be required at an additional cost of £575. These measures were immediately necessary, but to effect a permanent repair extensive relining had to be carried out. The work, at an estimated cost of £3,247, was authorised on 6 May 1910. It involved building an entirely new arch of blue bricks, 9in thick, throughout the tunnel, except for about 26yd about 100yd from the west end.

Work began on 12 June 1910 by lowering the track throughout to give sufficient headway for the shields used, and on 3 August the relining was begun. About forty men were employed throughout every night until the job was finished on 20 October. To avoid having to obtain the electric train staff, an occupation instrument was installed in a hut at the Bewdley end, with telephone communication with Bewdley South and Kidderminster Junction boxes. After the last booked

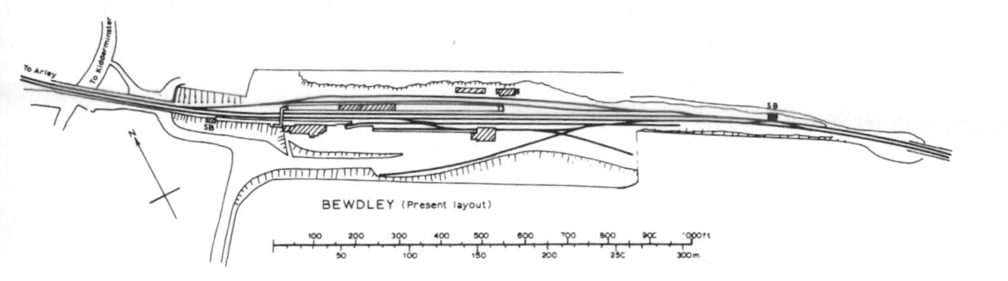

train had passed, about 22.15, the foreman would withdraw the occupation key, upon its being released by the signalmen, to ensure that no train or engine could enter the section. At 6.30 each morning all scaffolding was removed and at 6.55 the occupation key was replaced in the instrument to enable a staff to be withdrawn for the first train at 7.10. Because of the defective nature of the existing brick lining, the new arch was not keyed into the old, but brick packing sections were built up to it at intervals of 5ft horizontally and 4ft vertically, and the space between the linings was filled with cement grout to form a solid lining at least 2ft thick.[11] It was fortunate that the original tunnel was built to a generous size so that even with the new lining it has a width of 17ft 6in. The tunnel is dry, and is straight for about a third of its length. It then curves to the right and emerges into heathland, within sight of the 'Devil's Spittleful', a large block of hard sandstone which has eroded more slowly than its surroundings and is now covered in trees. Near here the Rifle Range Halt was opened in June 1905, like Foley Park, in connection with the rail-motor service. It was authorised at a cost of £145 on 12 April. The line continues to curve to the right round the south of what is now the West Midlands Safari Park, which was opened on 16 April 1973. In the angle just before the junction, on the left, the ground was excavated to rail level in 1986 to provide filling for the Bewdley by-pass. The 'loop' is just over 3 miles long.

At Bewdley, $5^1/_2$ miles from Hartlebury, considerable

excavation was necessary to form a site for the station. Before the SVR opened the Tenbury and Kidderminster lines were already authorised and the station was planned as a junction. Even so, with the approaching completion of the Kidderminster loop the island platform had to be enlarged, a shelter provided and a footbridge built: authorised on 19 December 1877 at a cost of £1,666. A further expenditure of £2,051 for extra sidings was approved on 9 August 1900. These included the 'Rock Siding' at the back of platform 3 and the siding along the far side of the yard. On 12 February 1896 the Traffic Committee sanctioned expenditure of £100 for additional toilet accommodation, and a corrugated iron lamp room, and on 1 May 1902 £680 for 'improvement in passenger accommodation', though what this was is not known. Various works around Bewdley station have been carried out by the present SVR. The locomotive inspection pit was completed in October 1974 and the water tanks at the south end, installed in the winter of 1973-4, were operational by July 1974. Changes were made also in the track layout and signalling at the north end to form a longer loop.

Bewdley, or Wribbenhall, viaduct, 112yd long, has seven arches turned in brick, 25ft span, with sandstone piers and spandrels, and a large skew arch over Kidderminster Road 48ft 9in span on the skew and 40ft on the square. Although half the Bewdley station area is cut into the sandstone and stands firmly on the rock, the viaducts north and south of it are off the rock and stand on alluvial deposit. Also, the local sandstone of which they are built weathers badly, and large areas of the piers and spandrels have had to be repaired in blue bricks, giving a patchy appearance.

Just north of Bewdley viaduct the line was crossed by a plate girder footbridge giving access from Northwood Lane to Summer Hill. Girder work for the bridge was authorised by the Engineering Committee on 15 March 1892. The bridge was removed in the 1930s but part of one of the piers can still be seen on the east side of the line. The Tenbury line paralleled the SVR for nearly a mile before diverging to the left.

Northwood Halt, $7^1/_4$ miles, was opened on 17 June 1935.[10]

North of here, the aqueduct from the Elan Valley is carried over the Severn on a segmental steel arch of 150ft span and 15ft rise. It is the lowest point on the aqueduct, and the pipes here carry a pressure of 250 psi. When the railway was under construction here a serious slip buried the rails. The line had to be rebuilt on the slipped material, and it was in this treacherous ground that the east abutment had to be built and the pipes laid. For the use of the contractors a siding, known as 'Folly Point Siding', was installed by the GWR on the left of the line, controlled by two ground frames each with two levers, locked by a key on the electric train staff for the section. It was inspected for the BoT by Lt Col G.W. Addison and passed on 16 September 1899. During construction of the aqueduct the railway was carried on timber baulks. Beneath the railway a chamber was built 47ft long and 45ft 9in wide. This and the bridge abutment were carried down to foundations 55 to 60ft below rail level. The GWR insisted on provision being made for doubling the railway on the right, away from the river. On completion of the aqueduct in 1906 the siding was removed. The roof of the chamber, steel troughing on steel joists, was removed in 1988–9 when it was filled in[12].

At Folly Point the line comes very close to the river, about 40ft above it. There has been trouble with slips here; the most recent in March 1980 involved excavation, insertion of stone crates and lifting the track about 18in over a length of 60ft. Trimpley reservoirs, on the left beyond here, were constructed in 1964 and commissioned in 1967. Their purpose, together with the pumping station on the right, is to regulate the abstraction of water from the Severn above here and to feed it into the Elan aqueduct. They have contributed greatly to control of flooding lower down. The cutting north of here has given trouble with slips over many years and constant attention is necessary to protect the line.

Immediately beyond the cutting the railway crosses the Severn on the Victoria Bridge which was fully described in chapter 4. At the inspection on 30 December 1861 the bridge was tested with three heavy locomotives (by the standards of the time) and a train of loaded wagons weighing one ton per foot run, and the deflection was only half an inch, considered by Yolland to be very satisfactory. In September 1979 the SVR undertook extensive repairs to the bridge. Scaffolding required 2 miles of steel tubes and $2^1/_2$ miles of planking. Royle & Stanley Ltd of Wolverhampton began cleaning the main girders. After the last train had crossed in late November the track was lifted and the ballast was removed by SVR workers. The timber deck was removed and the old timber joists were replaced by steel joists by Rubery Owen Steelwork Ltd. The work required fifty-four new beams, 6 tons of plates to renew the top flanges of the main girders, and 3,500 badly corroded rivets were replaced by high-tensile friction-grip bolts. The entire bridge was repainted using 1,200 litres or 264 gallons of paint. The track was relaid by SVR men and the work was completed in time for reopening on 1 March 1980. The total cost of the works was £94,346 towards which the SVR had a grant of £22,278 from the Ancient Monuments Secretariat of the Department of the Environment.[13]

Arley Station , $9^1/_4$ miles, originally had one platform on the right. The second, down, platform and extra siding accommodation, at a cost of £1,122 which included signalling installations described in chapter 8, was authorised on 3 August 1882. The works were inspected and sanctioned for the BoT by Col Rich in June 1883. On 9 November 1892 the Traffic Committee approved the provision of a ladies' waiting room and wc at a cost of £240. In 1901 an extra bedroom was built onto the station master's house at a cost of £65. Lengthening of the platforms, at the north end, widening the up platform, and alterations to the sidings, at a total cost of £508, were approved by the Traffic Committee on 12 December 1906. The work was completed in the summer of 1907. Arley was one of the sites selected by the GWR for a camping coach, in 1938.

After closure by BR in 1963 the up line through the station and the signals were removed. The signal box was dismantled by SVR members, thinking it would not be needed, and the lever frame and other equipment were transferred to Bridgnorth. Restoration began in 1971 and the station was reopened on 18 May 1974. The up line and sidings were replaced and a LNWR signal box, transferred from Yorton between Shrewsbury and Whitchurch, was re-erected with a GWR frame on the site of the old one. Signals were installed and the 'new' signal box was brought into use on 10 April 1976. The bracket home signal was transferred from Bewdley North when the layout there was rearranged in 1976. Arley won the 'Best Restored Station Award' for 1983.[14] Half a mile north of Arley the line enters Shropshire and also the Wyre Forest coalfield.

It was reported to the board on 5 June 1878 that the Billingsley Colliery Co was sinking a pit at Billingsley, and proposed to connect it to the SVR by a branch railway down the valley of the Borle Brook. The colliery company sought permission to construct sidings on land beside the SVR and agreed to pay the cost of a junction, estimated at £140, and also to pay for locking and signalling. The 14-year agreement was sealed on 29 August 1878 but the branch was not built until later. Another colliery was begun by the Highley Mining Co at Kinlet nearby in 1892, and on 3 April 1895 the GWR board agreed to provide a siding connection at a cost of £326 to be paid for by the mining company. On 9 October, Col Yorke, the BoT inspector, sanctioned the use of the siding which made a single south-facing connection to the main line. In 1898 the GWR entered into the first of several contracts for coal from Kinlet colliery. The sidings were greatly enlarged in 1899, the cost, about £1,300, being recovered from the Highley Mining Co over a period of three years. They were connected to a 320yd long loop off the main line, controlled by a ground frame at each end, Kinlet Sidings South GF on the right at 142 miles 3.9ch, and North GF on the left at 142 miles 9ch.

In 1911 an application was received from the New Billingsley Colliery Co for siding accommodation. It was agreed to provide this at the point where the Kinlet traffic was dealt with, and the expenditure of £2,805 for engineering and £1,665 for signalling, total £4,470 plus £100 for extra land was approved on 9 August. It included £688, the value of existing materials in the Kinlet colliery sidings. The new Billingsley Colliery Co agreed to pay £1,000 towards the cost of the works, the amount to be refunded by a rebate on their traffic. A new signal box was opened in December 1913 to control the sidings, as mentioned in chapter 8. The Billinglsey railway was $3^1/_2$ miles long and included a reversal a mile from the upper terminus.

Billingsley colliery closed on 18 September 1921, but the railway up the Borle valley was used for a number of years afterwards to serve a land-sale wharf at its terminus by the Bridgnorth - Cleobury Mortimer road, at the foot of an inclined tramway from Billingsley colliery. Kinlet colliery closed in 1935 and both colliery lines were dismantled sometime before 1941. A wagon repair works was established near the junction by the Highley Mining Co.[15] The signal box was closed in March 1943 and was replaced by two ground frames, one at each end of the loop, locked by the electric train token for the Arley-Highley section. There was also an intermediate token instrument in a cabin in the middle of the loop, with telephone communication on the Worcester - Bridgnorth omnibus circuit. A train could be placed in the loop and locked inside by inserting the token into this instrument. Another token could then be obtained from one end of the section.

From Highley to Ironbridge the GWR was in constant litigation concerning mining beneath the railway. As a general rule mineral rights would be leased by the major landowner to a mining company, which would assume responsibility for damage caused to buildings and other structures by subsidence. To avoid heavy legal costs and the possibility of being unable to prove that the subsidence was caused by the mining, and also waste of time and expense of repairs, a railway company would sometimes purchase the minerals beneath a section of railway to maintain support for a viaduct, station or other structure or length of track.

Borle viaduct, the next structure on the line, is built in sandstone throughout. It is 42yd long and consists of four arches of 25ft span. In 1915 the extension of mining activities by the Highley Mining Co was beginning to threaten the railway and on 9 October the GWR made an arrangement with the mining company for mineral support to be left beneath the railway particularly at Highley station and beneath Borle viaduct. On payment by the mining company of £74 16s 3d and a wayleave of £1 10s 0d per foot on coal under this area the mining company was allowed to drive two headings beneath the railway to work the Brooch coal. In 1976-7, with the assistance of the Manpower Services Commission, Borle viaduct was extensively rebuilt and tie bars were inserted.

Between Borle viaduct and Highley a serious slip during 1912 involved the GWR in acquiring over $1^1/_2$ acres of land for dealing with it. Just before Highley station the line crossed the lane by an iron bridge. The cast-iron girders bearing the railings carry the inscription 'Brymbo 1861'. The main girders were replaced in 1974. This was one of several SVR bridges for which ironwork was cast at Brymbo Ironworks near Wrexham.

Highley station, 11 miles 48ch, has always had only one platform, on the 'up' or east side of the line. There was one siding leading off from a point south of the station. Evidently there was some traffic in cattle because, on 1 December 1869, the GWR board approved the erection of a cattle pen, at a cost of £15. A Mr Baker of Kidderminster worked a stone quarry opposite the station. In 1880 a siding was provided to his quarry, Mr Baker paying the cost, about £53, and rent of £5 per annum for wayleave. The siding left the loop on the station siding by a junction facing north and curved sharply round to the quarry. The siding became disused following the death of Baker about 1881. Additional siding and platform accommodation, at a cost of £706.15s, was approved by the board on 3 August 1882, resulting in the present layout. The new works including the signal box and interlocking were sanctioned by Col Rich on behalf of the BoT on 25 June 1883.

Highley colliery, up the lane from the station, was in production by 1875. Rail access at Highley station was gained by a siding across the road. Wagons reached the colliery by a rope-worked incline, the lower half of which was single line and the upper half, above the passing place, three rails. Following the opening of Alveley colliery, the coal was mined from there and Highley colliery was closed for winding coal in 1940, being retained for ventilation and for winding men until final closure on 6 November 1968.

In 1901 a new bedroom was added to the station house, at a cost of £97 and in 1904 improvements in office and waiting room accommodation were approved at a cost of £674. Traffic on the SVR line at this period was heavy. On 12 February 1908 the general manager, J.C. (later Sir James) Inglis, recommended that crossing facilities and additional siding accommodation should be provided at Highley at an estimated cost of £6,960 for engineering and signalling, plus £200 for extra land. Evidently the outlay was not considered justified; the work was not undertaken and so it has never been possible to cross trains of passengers at Highley.

Access to the station by foot was down a path from the road from the village, and over a foot crossing. On 26 April 1912 the Traffic Committee approved the provision of a footbridge from the path, over the railway and down steps to the platform, and also a siding for horse boxes, at a total cost of £845. An additional £84 for foundations for the footbridge was approved on 9 July 1914. The footbridge was a steel lattice-girder structure of two spans. After closure of the station in 1963 it deteriorated to a dangerous condition and it was reluctantly demolished by SVR men in 1974. The ex LNWR water tower, from Whitchurch in Shropshire, was erected by the station staff and was first used on 20 June 1981. The horse box siding originally terminated behind the signal box. It was extended by the SVR in 1987, the work again being carried out mainly by the station staff. Highley won the 'Best Preserved Station Award' in 1982. A spell at Highley station on a warm summer afternoon is a delightful experience.

Highley platform stands on a curve to the right of 18 chains radius. Beyond the station, on a rising gradient of 1 in 100, the line curves to the left on a 20 chain radius curve followed, at mile 12 by a 17 chain curve to the left, the sharpest on the whole route. This is immediately followed by another 18 chain curve to the right. It was along here that the planned course of the line had to be changed because of a severe slip, resulting in this tortuous section.

Across the river, Alveley colliery opened in 1939. It was connected to the SVR, originally by a narrow-gauge cable-worked tramway, and later by an aerial ropeway, over a pleasing concrete arch bridge built by Thomas Beighton Ltd between June 1936 and June 1937, which is just visible from the railway. Coal screens and sidings were built beside the SVR on the right and there was also a halt for colliery workers, on the left, a bare stone platform 100ft long. Access to the sidings was controlled by two ground frames, North and South, on the left. The colliery closed on 31 January 1969 and the sidings were subsequently dismantled. They were unsuitable for storage of SVR stock because of the high risk of vandalism.

Hampton Loade station, 13$^3/_4$ miles, originally had only one platform on the west, or left, side, and a short siding opposite. At first it was named Hampton, but for less than a month. In *Bradshaw*, March 1862, it was Hampton Loade, and has been ever since. The expenditure of £1,177 for the up platform and passing loop was authorised on 3 August 1882 and the new works were passed for the BoT by Col Rich in June 1883. At the north end the space between the tracks becomes extremely narrow and great care has to be taken to ensure that a train is clear in the main line or loop before another is allowed to enter. Hampton Loade was also the site of a camping coach before the war. The girders of the underbridge just beyond the station were renewed in June 1975. Across the river, Hampton Loade Forge was the only tinplate works in Shropshire, in production from the 1820s to closure in 1866. A ferry, once chain operated, now works by the river current.

Sterns landslip south of Eardington has given trouble throughout the existence of the railway as the upper strata

EARDINGTON

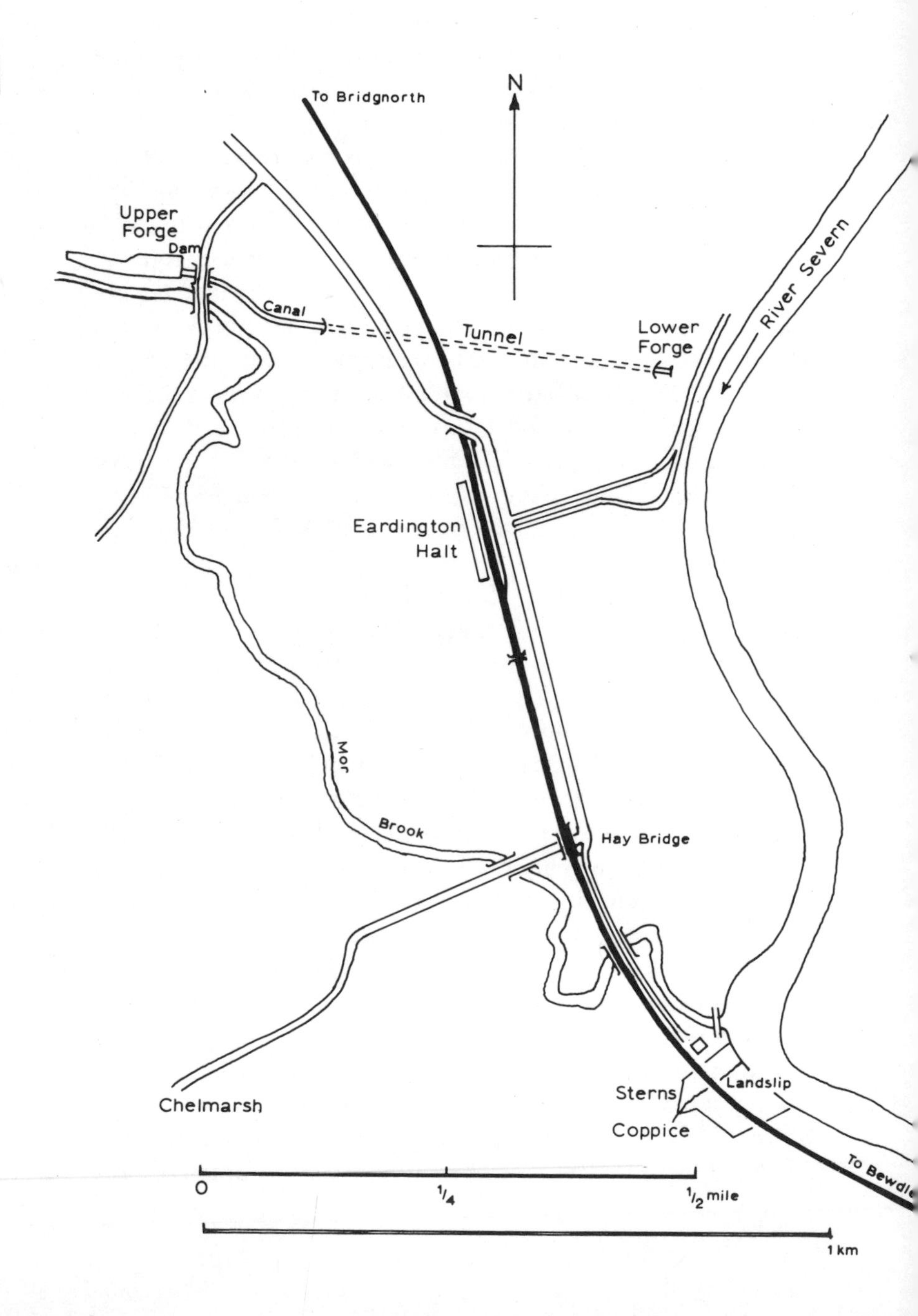
To Bridgnorth
N
Upper
Forge
Dam
Canal
Tunnel
Lower
Forge
River Severn
Eardington
Halt
Mor
Brook
Hay Bridge
Chelmarsh
Sterns
Coppice
Landslip
To Bewdl
0
1/4
1/2 mile
1 km

of clay slides towards the river. It is constantly on the move, entailing frequent slewing and packing of track. In February 1979 a serious slip cost £7,000 to remedy. A permanent speed restriciton of 5mph is in operation over the area. Just beyond here the line is carried over the Mor brook by an impressive brick arch. In a short distance the line crosses a road at The Hay. The main girders of this bridge were renewed in June 1975. In summer 1984 one of the outer girders was damaged by a lorry. Further extensive repairs were carried out early in 1987.

Beyond a cutting is Eardington Halt, 16 miles, sited to serve the Upper and Lower Forges. Upper Forge in the Mor Brook valley, reached from the station along the lanes, was built in 1777-8 and was connected to the Lower Forge by a navigable canal tunnel 750yd long, 9ft wide and 6ft high, passing under the railway 550yd north of the station. The tunnel terminated in a large cave cut in the sandstone cliff above the river where there are numerous remains of the Lower Forge. In 1864 it was proposed to build a long siding to the Lower Forge, at an estimated cost of £800. William Orme Foster, owner and manager of the works, offered to advance £500 towards the cost, the railway company agreeing to pay the remaining £300 out of capital, but the work was never carried out. The station platform was extended in 1893, at a cost of £130, but only six years later, in 1899, the ironworks closed and plant and materials were removed to Stourbridge. The remains of the Upper and Lower Forges form a fascinating site for the industrial archaeologist and are well worth a visit.

Eardington Halt was much used during the early years of the present SVR as an intermediate stopping place with watering facilities. After being pleasingly restored, it was closed in connection with the proposed rebuilding to form a future terminus (see chapter 9). Later it was rebuilt and reopened on 7 March 1981 but was little used and it last appeared in the SVR timetable, as a request stop, in 1982. It is now out of use and part of the platform where it collapsed has been cut back. The siding is used by the permanent way department. Minor slips have occurred near Eardington from time to time.

A quarter of a mile north of Eardington Halt a track crosses the line. It formerly connected the Upper and Lower Forges. On 17 March 1869 the board authorised 'repairing, whitewashing and papering' the cottage at the crossing at a cost of £6. At the $148^{3}/_{4}$ milepost is Eardington summit, 210ft above sea level. From here the line drops at 1 in 100 through a sandstone cutting to Knowle Sands tunnel, 40yd 2ft long, of double track width with a segmental arch roof 25ft span. Knowle Sands siding, on the left, served a brickworks. Oldbury viaduct just beyond here, in red brick with a sandstone parapet, has five arches of 33ft span. It was substantially rebuilt in 1975-6. Just below, on the right, hardly seen by the railway passenger, is Daniels Mill with its water wheel still in position. Alan George, the owner, was one of the founder members of the SVR Society (Chapter 9).

The Bridgnorth by-pass, opened on 29 March 1985, can now be seen on the right, its concrete spans striding across the river. The railway is carried over it on a through plate-girder bridge of 77ft 3in span, 17ft between girders, with a concrete floor. Details of the construction of the bridge are given in chapter 9, p189. Beyond here the line crosses the Cleobury road by a plate girder bridge with a span of 55ft on the skew and 35ft on the square. It was renewed by the SVR in autumn 1978.

Bridgnorth station, $18^{1}/_{4}$ miles, has always had two platforms. On 12 May 1887, following a suggestion from the town clerk, it was agreed to improve the passenger facilities

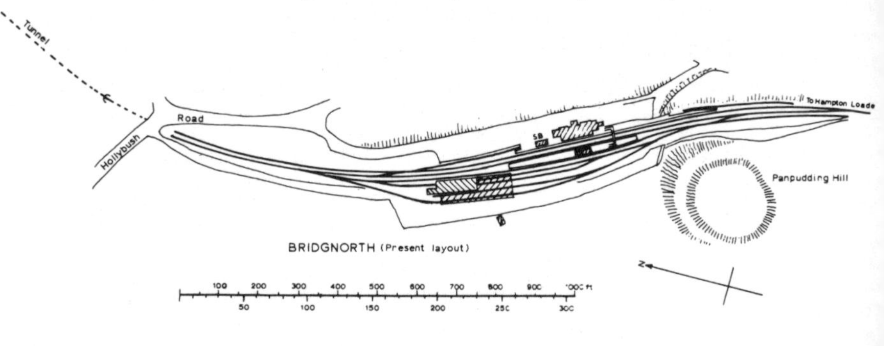

BRIDGNORTH (Present layout)

by raising both platforms, lengthening the down platform and providing it with a waiting room, and erecting a footbridge. A new approach road was built at the expense of Bridgnorth corporation.

On 16 February 1865 the Traffic Committee stated that a crane was 'much required' at Bridgnorth, and directed that a spare one at Stourport should be removed at a cost of £50. Further work was authorised on 13 August 1891 including siding accommodation, extension of the roadway alongside the coal siding and the construction of a retaining wall. These works were passed by Major Marindin for the BoT on 26 October 1892.

Passengers at Bridgnorth station a hundred years ago, as today, found the journey on foot between station and town somewhat strenuous. Bridgnorth corporation decided to ease matters by building a long footbridge from opposite the station entrance, over Hollybush Road, to New Road (opened in 1786), up into the town. On 2 May 1895 the GWR board granted permission for the corporation to construct an abutment for the footbridge by the station. The bridge, built by Alfred Owen & Partners in 1895, consisted of four steel lattice spans. Under agreements dated 2 May 1895 and 10 August 1946 with Bridgnorth Borough Council, the council covenanted to inspect and to maintain the bridge and to indemnify the railway company against loss, injury or damage. The GWR was to pay half the cost of repairs and repainting. Unfortunately, following closure of the railway by BR in 1963 the bridge was allowed to deteriorate. In 1967 the Council decided to demolish the bridge but this was delayed and in 1969 a public appeal was launched to save the footbridge and £1,500 was raised. This, together with £2,000 already offered, was hopelessly inadequate to repair or to replace the bridge. On 30 September 1970 the bridge was closed and the ends were boarded up. On 1 April 1974 Bridgnorth was demoted to rural borough status and so lost its powers as a highway authority and also its powers to spend on the upkeep of the bridge. Later in that year it was sold to the SVR for a

GRADIENTS. SHREWSBURY TO BRIDGNORTH

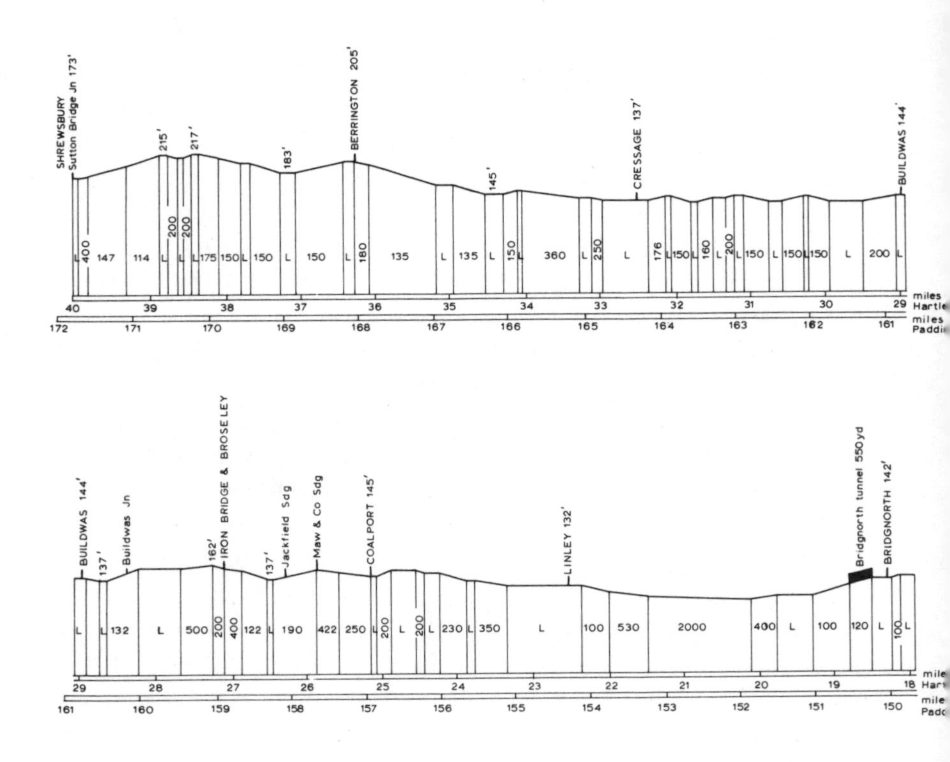

nominal sum of £1. The object was then to rebuild it at a cost of £15,000 after which its maintenance would be taken over by Salop County Council. The latter, with Rubery Owen Holdings Ltd, successors to the construction firm, undertook to pay £1,000 each towards the cost of repair. However, with so many other pressing commitments, the SVR was unable to raise the £24,900 which, it was discovered, would be the cost of repair. After further discussion it was conceded that there was no hope for the bridge, and in 1976 it was dismantled. A footbridge here is much needed and there has been talk of erecting a new one.

On 9 January 1901 the general manager of the GWR, Sir

Joseph Loftus Wilkinson, stated that siding accommodation at Bridgnorth was inadequate and he proposed a further siding to hold forty-seven wagons, the cost of £3,330 including improvements to signalling but excluding land. Further cattle accommodation at a cost of £78 was approved on 31 May 1905. More work has been carried out by the SVR. The new locomotive shed was started in March 1976 and was completed in 1977. It contains an illuminated inspection pit, and a set of heavy lifting jacks from London Transport. The new shed adjoined the old goods shed which has been made into a well-equipped machine shop where the heaviest work can be undertaken, including wheel turning. From November 1980 to summer 1981 the up platform was extended by 200ft to a total length of 519ft. Materials were obtained from two old GWR platforms, at Cradley Heath between Stourbridge and Birmingham, and from Acocks Green between Birmingham and Leamington. During the work the foundations of the old north signal box were uncovered.

Immediately north of Bridgnorth station the line passed beneath the High Town in a tunnel 550yd long, on a double curve, first to the right then to the left. The original bore was 16ft 8in wide at the south end and 19ft at the north, and 16ft high. On 17 March 1911 a recommendation by the Engineering Committee for relining the tunnel at a total estimated cost of £4,078 was approved by the board. The cost included £110 to the signal department, presumably for the wire to the up distant. The tunnel was relined with vertical walls, reducing the width to 15ft to within a few yards of each end.

Beyond the tunnel the river was followed fairly closely, with views of Apley Park and House on the right. Linley station, 22½ miles, served the Apley estate and had no public road access. The goods siding, on the left, was closed on 10 September 1951 and the station reduced to a halt. The suspension bridge over the river connected the house to the station, and replaced a ferry. It was built by David Rowell & Co, Westminster, in 1905. Just over 1¾ miles beyond here the line crossed a track by a substantial segmental arch in stone.

As the line approached Coalport it entered the Severn Gorge and the mining and industrial section. On the right a siding trailed in from the Coalport Brick & Tile Works. Just beyond here was the entrance to the Coalport loop 1476ft long, the longest on the line. Coalport station, 25$^{1}/_{4}$ miles, originally had one platform on the 'up' or north side. On 28 February 1894 the general manager, Henry Lambert, proposed that, in conjunction with signalling improvements required by the BoT, the station should be made a crossing place with the addition of a second platform and further siding accommodation for Exley's tile traffic, at a total cost of £4,062. On 22 January 1896 the new works were given BoT sanction by Col Yorke. The expenditure of £84 for an additional bedroom on the stationmaster's house was approved on 27 May 1903.

At Jackfield, 25$^{1}/_{2}$ miles, a siding was provided for Maw & Co at that company's expense. Its use was sanctioned by Major Marindin for the BoT in 1877. On 13 March 1889 the Engineering Committee approved an arrangement with William Orme Foster, of Apley House, for the purchase from him, for £400, of his interest in tile clay and minerals under the SVR at Jackfield, and also of the cottages and land adjoining, Mr Foster giving up his rights as user of the pit shaft on the site. The sidings at Jackfield were extended in 1890 at a cost of £220, and an additional siding was provided for Maw & Sons, as the firm had then become, for £130 paid for by Maw. A siding extension and provision of a wharf for Prestage & Co's traffic, at a cost of £290, was approved on 29 November 1905. Prestage would pay a rent of £15 per annum for twenty years. On 15 July 1908 the GWR approved an arrangement under which Maw & Sons would work the firebrick and tile clay under two pieces of land belonging to and adjoining the railway at Jackfield in return for leaving unworked the clay beneath the railway itself.

In August 1883 Messrs J.A. & E.G. Exley gave notice to the GWR that they intended to work a seam of clay under the SVR near Jackfield, the seam about 15ft thick and 90ft below the rails. The GWR tried to negotiate for the purchase of the clay below the railway but the terms asked by Messrs Exley were so excessive that the GWR decided to allow them to proceed, and if the workings were found to affect the railway seriously then blocks of clay would be purchased from time to time. J. Ward Armstrong, district engineer, Hereford, proposed to secure the line by 'a strong grid-iron of timber' which, he said, could be re-used if the company decided eventually to purchase the clay. On 24 March 1886 it was reported that Exley's offered to leave unworked such a quantity of clay as was considered necessary to support the railway and also the sulphur coal and other minerals above the clay, amounting to about two acres, at the rate of £1,000 an acre, but Armstrong considered that there would be little difficulty in maintaining the line, and so the offer was declined. A subsidence did occur by the line on 25 November 1887 but Armstrong considered that there was no danger to traffic.

In 1891 Exley & Sons started erecting a large brick and tile works near Coalport SVR station, and in May they notified the GWR of their intention to work a bed of clay 25ft thick 90ft below the railway. On 18 June the GWR entered into an agreement with Exley's for coal to be left under the railway, and not to work other minerals over an area of about 8 acres within 30 yards of the perpendicular below the rails. In return the GWR undertook to construct a siding at a cost of £228 and to lend Exley's, free of charge, materials for extending the siding for 550 yards.

A halt was opened at Jackfield, 25¾ miles, on 3 December 1934. Largely as a result of the clay mining over a long period, a severe landslip developed here at the end of 1951 and went on moving at the rate of about 6ins a day until early 1952 by which time the line had been pushed a total of 25ft sideways and downwards. Over 1,000 tons of cinders were absorbed over a 400yd stretch in restoring the track. A new halt was opened on 1 March 1954 to replace the first damaged in the slip. Exley's brick and tile works closed in 1956. Since the railway closed, subsidence and slipping have continued. The adjacent road was so badly damaged that it had to be abandoned and rebuilt on the old track bed. This also has collapsed and the road is now made of two chains of wooden slats. The site of Maw's works has been developed as the Jackfield Tile Museum. The gates at the level crossing near Jackfield, still in existence, must have been among the longest on any single line. Just beyond here the line crossed a track by another Brymbo iron bridge.

Ironbridge & Broseley, 27$^1/_4$ miles, was a crossing station from the opening of the line. On the recommendation of the general manager on 30 October 1895 the name was changed to Iron Bridge & Broseley on 9 November, but the reason is obscure. Although the Ordnance Survey continues to print Iron Bridge, the town and museum are Ironbridge. On 5 October 1898 the Traffic Committee approved the provision of a telephone between Iron Bridge station, Jackfield siding and Messrs Maw's siding at an estimated cost of £22. Maws were to pay half the maintenance cost. An additional goods siding was ordered to be provided at Iron Bridge, at a cost of £90, on 8 April 1908. The road across the famous iron bridge, just below the station, passed over a level crossing at the north end of the platforms. Beyond here the line traversed the steeply sloping valley side on a viaduct of ten segmental arches of 25ft 6in span, constructed in brick on stone piers. It is a rare example in Britain of a viaduct built into the hillside.

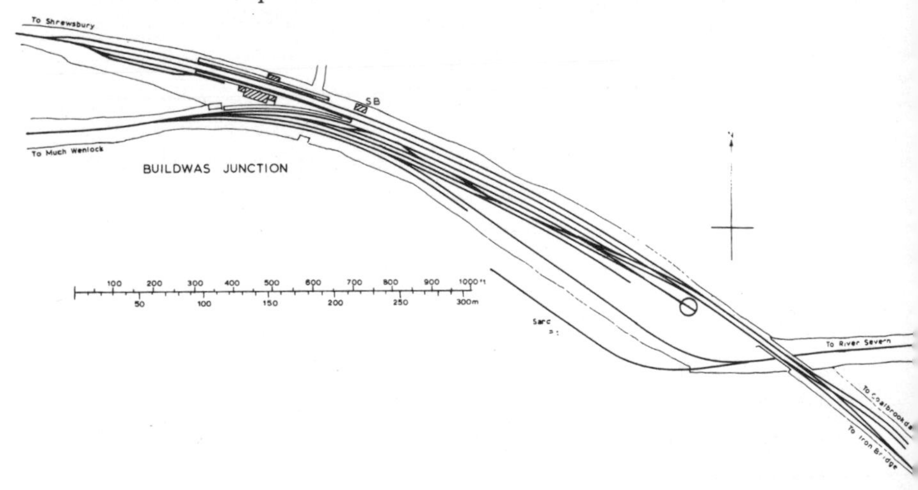

A slip in the cutting near here in 1922 involved work costing £1,310 to make it safe.

On the approach to Buildwas the double-track line from Coalbrookdale came in on the right across the Albert Edward Bridge, and the Much Wenlock line turned off to the left, and immediately began climbing to its own platform at a higher level at Buildwas station, 28 $^{1}/_{2}$ miles. This always had two platforms for the SVR and one for the Much Wenlock line. On 10 May 1899 the Traffic Committee agreed to provide a siding here to serve Mr Griffith's sand fields, at an estimated cost of £138, to be paid by him. He was also to pay one penny per ton in addition to the ordinary rates for working the traffic into and out of the siding. The loop at Buildwas was lengthened in 1904.

A new power station came into use here in 1932, involving the construction of extensive sidings and a new signal box. Today the greatly extended power station is served only by the Coalbrookdale line from Madeley Junction on the Shrewsbury - Wolverhampton line.

At Buildwas the SVR left the gorge section, passed close to Buildwas Abbey, on the right, and entered the flat country on the bed of the ancient pre-glacial lake. The Severn, in its numerous meanders, came close to the railway at several points. Cressage, deriving its name from 'Christsache', from the Saxon 'ache' for oak, had a station at 32 $^{1}/_{2}$ miles, with one platform and a siding on the 'up' or north side. Improvements to the stationmaster's house, at a cost of £50, were authorised in 1888. The construction of a loop and down platform with waiting shed, and extension of the up platform at a cost of £671 was approved on 14 June 1893. The works were passed for the BoT by Major Yorke on 14 July 1894.[16] An additional bedroom was built onto the stationmaster's house in 1901, at a cost of £78.

At Cound, 33 $^{3}/_{4}$ miles, a halt was opened on 4 August 1934, close to a ferry over the river. Beyond here, at 34 miles 45ch, the line crossed the Cound Brook by a bridge of two segmental arches of 25ft span. Arches were turned in brick, with facing rings, piers and spandrels in stone. An overbridge beyond here was constructed of cast-iron girders, again 'Brymbo 1860'.

Berrington, 36 miles 9ch, like Cressage, originally had only an up platform and one siding on the same side. The loop, down platform with shelter, and extension of the up platform were authorised at the same time as at Cressage, at a cost of £1,068, and they were passed by Major Yorke on the same day; but at Berrington he required a ladies' waiting room and wc to be provided on the up platform. The general manager approved an expenditure of £240 for this, on 8 August 1894. At 38 miles 30ch the SVR reached its summit level of 217ft.

On 13 August 1866 the ramshackle Potteries, Shrewsbury & North Wales Railway, the 'Potts', was opened to its Shrewsbury terminus at Abbey Foregate, with connections to Shrewsbury Joint station and the Shrewsbury & Birmingham. It crossed over the SVR about a quarter of a mile south of the junction with the Shrewsbury & Hereford. Its history does not concern us here, but in 1911 it was reopened by Col Stephens as the Shropshire & Montgomeryshire Railway. When it was finally closed in 1960 BR built a spur up to it from the SVR to serve a new oil depot at the Abbey station, and the bridge over the SVR was removed. The connection was controlled by a ground frame unlocked by the section token. Until July 1988 the connection between here and Sutton Bridge Junction was all that was left of the SVR at the northern end. Trains of up to ten vehicles were propelled from Sutton Bridge Junction or Abbey station. It is now closed.

In accordance with the requirements of the BoT, junctions of single lines, either with other single lines or with double lines, were made double junctions. On the SVR the divergence into double line was 18 chains south of Sutton Bridge Junction, just north of the bridge under the 'Potts' line. It was certainly so in 1882 because it is shown on the OS 1 : 2500 map of that date. It was protected by the home and starting signals, but how the points were operated so far from the box is not known. They were probably weighted. On 1 January 1894, as will be explained in chapter 8, these points became

Burnt Mill Junction when a signal box was opened on the left. On the right just beyond here was a three-road carriage shed 475ft long. At Sutton Bridge Junction, Shrewsbury, 39 miles 71ch, the SVR joined the Shrewsbury & Hereford Railway. The junction had earlier been known as Coleham, and then Severn Valley Junction. From here it was a run of just over half a mile to Shrewsbury station, 40¾ miles from Hartlebury.

CHAPTER 7

The Wolverhampton - Bridgnorth Projects

No history of the SVR would be complete without reference to the various projected railways between Bridgnorth and Wolverhampton. Bridgnorth has always leaned towards Wolverhampton; the towns are only 14 miles apart and the country between, while offering nothing in the way of traffic, presents no great difficulties to railway construction. The principal obstruction to a railway was Wolverhampton itself: the railway stations were on the north-east side and Bridgnorth is south of west. A railway would have to go through or under the town centre, or round the north or south, thereby increasing the cost and distance. All the routes projected were considerably longer than the direct road. The routes are shown on the map on p115.

Altogether nine bills were prepared and of these only two received Royal Assent. The first to be advertised was the Wolverhampton & Bridgenorth (sic) Railway project of 1860. No engineer's name appears on the plan.[1] The line was to leave the Shrewsbury & Birmingham Railway 3 miles from Wolverhampton station and was to pass through Wergs, Pattingham and Worfield to join the intended line of the SVR about 2 miles north of Bridgnorth. The section showed a ruling gradient of 1 in 65 down from mile $4^1/_2$ from Wolverhampton for $1^1/_2$ miles, and $1^1/_4$ miles of 1 in 70 down from mile $6^3/_4$. The total length

Notes to this chapter are on p217 .

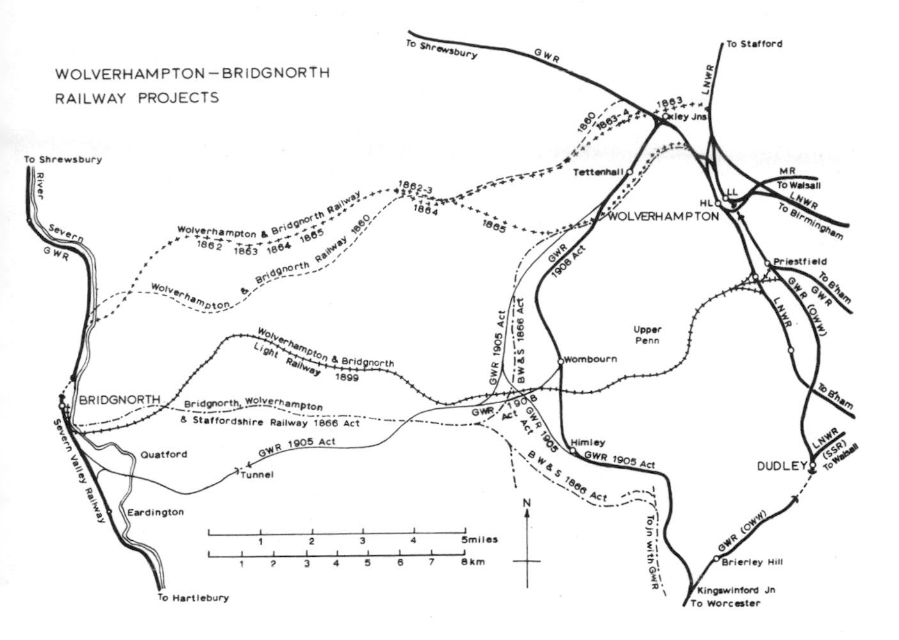

was 12 miles 3f. There was insufficient interest in it and the bill was never presented in Parliament.

A plan to connect Bridgnorth to the Black Country south of Wolverhampton appeared in 1861 when a plan and section were deposited for the South Staffordshire & Central Wales Railway Dudley and Bridgenorth (sic). The drawings[2] were prepared by Richard Taylor, 'Bridgenorth'. He can hardly be blamed for the spelling because it is so spelt on the 1 inch OS map of the time. The engineers were McClean & Stileman of Westminster. The line, 16 miles 3.5f long, left the South Staffordshire Railway (leased to the LNWR 1 February 1861) at Dudley, passed through a tunnel 600yd long, passed a mile south of Himley, a mile south of Claverley and ended a mile south of Bridgnorth. Clearly until the SVR was built the last half mile could not be finalised.

A second Wolverhampton & Bridgnorth scheme appeared in 1862, prepared by John Addison. He was born in Liverpool on 12 April 1820 and he spent much of his time on railways in northern England and southern Scotland. From 1857 until he retired in 1884 he was manager of the Maryport & Carlisle Railway and it was during this period that he superintended the surveys. He died at Maryport on 22 March 1903. Addison's line was similar to that of 1860, but from Pattington it passed 2 miles north of Worfield. At the Wolverhampton end it was to make a junction with the Shrewsbury & Birmingham and also to continue to the GJR near Bushbury.[3] By this time the SVR was open and more interest was shown. The bill was presented in Parliament by Viscount Newport on 6 February 1863 but on the 23rd it was decided that the preamble was not proved and it was thrown out. It was presented again in February 1864 but it was withdrawn by the promoting parties on 27 April. A third attempt was made in the 1865 session, this time without the extension to the GJR, but again it was withdrawn by the promoters, on 10 May.[4] Addison worked out a new scheme in 1865. This was to leave the Shrewsbury & Birmingham south of the Oxley viaduct and follow the Staffordshire & Worcestershire Canal for 3½ miles, then to turn westwards to join the routes of 1862-3-4 near Pattingham.[5] This was not even presented in Parliament.

At the same time another project, the Bridgnorth, Wolverhampton & Staffordshire Railway[6] was prepared by the engineer J. Fogerty. This was a combination of two schemes. From a junction with the Shrewsbury & Birmingham just west of Oxley viaduct it followed a similar line to the previous project but continued southwards to Wombourn. Here it was to turn westwards via Halfpenny Green, across the Seven on a viaduct 130yd long near Oldbury, to join the SVR just south of Bridgnorth station, 16 miles 4.67f. The ruling gradient was 1 in 60. A branch (Rly No 2) from a west-facing junction near Wombourn was to form a connection with the Kingswinford branch of the former OWW, by then the GWR, about 4 miles. Out of this was another branch of just over a mile to Swindon (Staffordshire). The bill was presented to Parliament on 8 February 1866 and went up to the Lords on 16 April where it was examined by the Select Committee on

7 June. Many witnesses gave evidence in support of the bill, including Henry Whitmore, then MP for Bridgnorth. He spoke of the difficulties of travel from the town as if the SVR did not exist. Other witnesses complained, justifiably, of the poor communication between Bridgnorth and the Black Country, and to London.

James Grierson, general manager of the GWR, gave evidence against the bill. He claimed that in the week 9-15 May there were 13 tons of goods, three parcels and ten passengers booked from Wolverhampton to Bridgnorth and 13 tons of goods, two parcels and sixteen passengers the other way. He regarded the proposed railway as part of an attempt by the LNWR to reach Wales. He said that when traffic justified it the GWR would build it, and he ignored the possibility that a more direct route might generate more traffic. In view of the circuitous railway journey via Wellington or Shrewsbury or Hartlebury his evidence was clearly absurd and the Committee decided that the preamble of the bill was proved. It received the Royal Assent on 28 June 1866 (c 129). The Act incorporating the company authorised capital of £270,000 and £90,000 on loan, and gave powers to construct 21 miles of railway.

The money was not forthcoming and the powers lapsed. Another line along nearly the same route, and with a connection with the LNWR near Dunstall, Wolverhampton, was surveyed by the engineers W.J. Kingsbury and T. Dowell in 1871.[7] The branches were omitted. The main line was 16½ miles long from the junction with the Shrewsbury & Birmingham to the junction with the SVR. There were two short tunnels, 212 yd and 150yd at 1 mile 6.5f and 3 miles 5.5f from the SVR, and the ruling gradient was again 1 in 60. The bill was presented in Parliament by William Henry Foster on 8 February 1872 but on 20 March it was thrown out because the preamble was not proved.

Here the matter remained for a while until the Light Railways Act of 1896 made a new approach possible. A completely new line, the Wolverhampton & Bridgnorth Light Railway, was planned by W.B. Myers-Beswick from junctions with both the GWR and LNWR near Priestfield south of Wolverhampton, and along a fairly direct route to join the SVR south of Bridgnorth station, and also to a separate station in Bridgnorth Lower Town.[8] The ruling gradient was 1 in 66; the total estimated cost of the main line and seven branches, amounting to 22 miles, was £311,073.

By now the possibility that the route might offer some traffic was beginning to penetrate to the GWR board at Paddington. At the meeting on 20 October 1904 J.C. Inglis, general manager and former chief engineer, explained why, in his opinion, it was desirable for the GWR to obtain powers in the next session of Parliament for a line from Wolverhampton to Bridgnorth. No reference is made in the minutes to what he said, but the board agreed and it was decided to prepare a bill.

The GWR scheme was roughly similar to the Bridgnorth, Wolverhampton & Staffordshire project of 1866 and 1872.[9] It consisted of a railway from two junctions with the Shrewsbury & Birmingham east and west of Oxley viaduct, following the S&W Canal to the west of Wombourn, then turning westwards, via Halfpenny Green and through open country, through a tunnel 333yd long, and over the Severn near Quatford to two junctions with the SVR 1 mile and 1$^1/_2$ miles south of Bridgnorth, length 15$^1/_4$ miles. A branch from a north-facing junction near Wombourn connected with the Kingswinford branch. The engineers were William Wylie Grierson (1863-1935), chief engineer of the GWR (whose father, as general manager, had opposed the 1866 scheme) and Edward Parry (1844-1920) who had been resident engineer on the Great Central main line from Annesley to Rugby. The GWR Act of 11 July 1905 (c 118) gave power to construct, as well as these lines, the line from Aynho Junction to Ashenden Junction, part of the direct Birmingham - Paddington line, and other lines in the Ealing and Hammersmith area of west London.

While the bill was being prepared, the GWR instituted a bus service between Wolverhampton Low Level station and Bridgnorth station using three Clarkson steam buses which the GWR bought at a cost of £900 each. They were exhibited at

Paddington and, on 4 November 1904, at Bridgnorth. After a ceremonial trip from Wolverhampton to Bridgnorth and back the next day, conveying civic dignitaries from Wolverhampton and officials of the GWR, the buses began the public service on 7 November. The journey took $1^1/_2$ hours, the buses travelling at 8mph.

During the following winter the buses gave considerable trouble, particularly on the Hermitage Hill out of Bridgnorth, and there were several minor accidents. At the end of March 1905 they were transferred to the Cheddar - Burnham service in Somerset and were replaced by Milnes - Daimler petrol buses from 1 April. Apart from their noise, these proved more reliable, but the journey still took $1^1/_2$ hours. They must have been well built and maintained, for they operated the service, providing four journeys each way, until January 1920, when they were replaced by AEC buses, but the journey time was still $1^1/_2$ hours. It could be quicker on a bicycle. On 2 June 1923 the service was taken over by Wolverhampton Corporation, and the journey time became $1^1/_4$ hours. It continued to improve during the 1920s and '30s. In 1969 the Wolverhampton buses were taken over by the West Midlands Passenger Transport Executive.[10]

Having established the bus service in 1904 the GWR did nothing about the railway under the 1905 Act. A revised scheme was authorised in the GWR (Additional Powers) Act of 1908 (c 25) bringing the junction with the Kingswinford line into Wombourn. Nothing further had been done when developments in the coalfield on Pensnett Chase caused the GWR to revise the scheme, and in 1913 the Bridgnorth line was postponed while work went ahead on the line through to Kingswinford. Construction was resumed after World War I and in the GWR (Additional Powers) act of 1924 (c 50) the time for completion of the Kingswinford section was extended to 18 December 1924 and for the Bridgnorth line to 1 October 1927. After the war the rapid development of road transport made it clear that the Bridgnorth line was no longer a viable proposition. The road service had become firmly established and with the country between Wombourn and Bridgnorth offering no traffic it was decided to abandon that portion of the railway. Work went ahead on the 'branch' which thus became the main line, and the 'Wombourn line' as it was known was opened for through traffic on 11 January 1925. A passenger service of steam railcars between Stourbridge Junction and Wolverhampton via Wombourn began on 11 May, but it was short-lived and was withdrawn on 31 October 1932. The Wombourn line was heavily used during World War II for freight traffic avoiding Wolverhampton and it continued in use as a freight route until 27 February 1965. It was officially closed as a through route on 1 March but it remained in use at the Kingswinford end.[11]

CHAPTER 8

Signalling and Operation

There were originally only five stations on the SVR at which trains could be crossed: Stourport, Bewdley, Bridgnorth, Ironbridge and Buildwas. Trains were worked by single-needle telegraph alone.[1] Signalling was primitive; an early picture of Bridgnorth station shows a semaphore signal with two arms, one on each side of the post. Signals were operated from levers on the platforms and controlled entry of the trains into the station. Departure into the single-line section was controlled by the telegraph only. Points were operated by individual levers at the lineside. Sidings had no safety points and wagons could be prevented from fouling the main line only by the use of scotch blocks.

Trains had hand brakes only; tender engines had no brakes whatever and could be stopped either by a hand brake on the tender or, in an emergency, by throwing them into reverse. Some tank engines had hand brakes, others no brakes. That there were so few accidents is a tribute to the care and diligence of the entire staff.

A slight collision which occurred at Bewdley on 8 November 1866 was mentioned in the Traffic Committee minutes on 14 November:

> The 4.00 pm Goods from Buildwas, notwithstanding that the signals were against it, ran into the station and came into contact with another goods train standing there.

Notes to this chapter will be found on p217.

Joseph Owen, the driver of the 6.35 pm train, was fined 5s for running at too fast a speed and Eli Lambert, a porter working as under-Guard, was fined 15s for not putting on his breaks (sic) when signalled to do so which omission was the main cause of the accident.

With the gradual introduction of continuous brakes on passenger trains, brakes on locomotives began to appear in 1876, largely to relieve the stress on drawbars when the train brakes were applied.

This was a period of great progress in the development of safety appliances for railways, but the speed of their adoption varied from one railway company to another. It was not until 1889 that the Regulation of Railways Act made compulsory the block system, interlocking of points and signals, and continuous brakes on passenger trains. On the GWR these improvements began to appear during the 1860s, first on the main lines and then on the secondary routes.

Lack of any connection between points and signals led to a collision at Bridgnorth on 7 May 1870 when a porter, Thomas Alfred James, turned some points in the wrong direction. He was noted as having 'a good character for steadiness and attention to duty' and he was allowed to return to his duties. A claim for £250 from a Miss Stormont, injured in the collision, was settled on 3 August for £100.

The following regulations, from the GWR working timetable of May - June 1872 show the method of operation by telegraph which was used until the introduction of train staff and ticket working.

REGULATIONS FOR SIGNALLING TRAINS ON THE SEVERN VALLEY LINE, AND FOR OBTAINING "LINE CLEAR"

The "block" or signal instruments are to be devoted exclusively to signalling of Trains, and the authority to work them is entrusted solely to the Station-master, or signalman in charge of the instruments and signals, without whose authority no signal whatever is to be passed.

In order to make these regulations more clearly intelligible, it is proposed to designate the station from which the train is to start as "Station A," the station to which the Train is about to proceed as "Station B".

1. Immediately previous to starting a train from Station A, the needle must be moved steadily to and fro, so as to call the attention of station B, to which the train is to proceed.

Station B will repeat the signal, to show his attention has been obtained.

Station A will then give three steady beats of his needle to the left, asking the question, "Is line clear?" If line is clear, station B will reply, "Yes, clear," by repeating the same number of beats also to the left.

Station A will, on receiving the above, reply by blocking over his needle to "Line clear," and keep it blocked over until the Train has left or passed his station, when he will immediately give the signal "Train started," by giving three steady and distinct beats on his needle to the right, upon which Station B will block the needle opposite to the words on the dial, "Train on line," and keep it blocked over till the Train has arrived at his station.

Immediately on the arrival of the train at station B, the signalman will remove the peg, after satisfying himself that the whole of the Train has arrived, and station A is to be advised of it by giving one steady beat of the needle to the left, which station A will acknowledge to station B in the same manner, signifying that the Train has arrived.

2. If, when the signal is given from Station A, "Is line clear?" the line should not be clear, the reply, "No, blocked," is to be immediately returned by Station B, by giving five distinct beats to the right, and the needle at B is then to be permanently blocked over to the right until line is clear, when the peg is to be removed and the instrument left free for a repetition of the inquiry.

3. On receiving the reply at station A, "No, blocked," it

will be the duty of the person in charge of the instrument at station A to watch the needle until it is released, and then the question, "Is line clear?" must be repeated from A to B; and under no circumstances whatever is the train to be started until the reply is received at A, "Yes, clear."

4. If, after giving the notice of a train's arrival, it should be necessary to obstruct the line, before doing so, the signalman must release the peg from "Line clear" and give five distinct beats on the needle to the right, to the signalman on either or both sides (as the case may be) which five beats are to be returned, and the needle must then be blocked over to "Train on line," and kept blocked over until the line is clear, when notice is to be returned in the same manner as after a train's arrival.

5. After the signal "Train started" has been given from A to B, and the station B has pegged the needle to the right, "Train on line," thc instrument is to be carefully watched until the needle is released.

6. The times at which "Is line clear?" and "Line clear," are sent and received, "Time of departure of Train," and time of receipt of signal "Train has arrived," are to be carefully entered in the "Line clear book" at the stations, and the signature of the Stationmaster or signalman placed opposite to the entries. The book must always be left open in a convenient position near the instrument. All entries must be made in ink, and no erasures with a knife will be allowed under any circumstances.

7. The stationmaster or signalman in charge at station B must, at all times, before he replies "Yes, clear," satisfy himself it is free, not only from the Ordinary Trains, but also from any Special Trains, Ballast Trains, Trucks, or other obstructions. He must also be sure that no Train has been divided and only part of it brought into the station, as may sometimes happen, with a heavy Goods Train.

8. Should the Block Telegraph be out of order, recourse must be had to the Single Needle Telegraph, and the following rules strictly observed:-

When a Train is ready to leave station A, the question in full is to be asked of station B, "Is line clear?" station B will reply (as the case may be) with "Yes, clear," or, "No, blocked," and the question and answer, with the times of asking, must be entered, in ink in the "Line clear book" at both stations. If the answer, "No, blocked," is returned to Station A, the Train must not be started from that station until another message is receive from station B that "Line is clear." Station A must then send a message to station B, "Train started," and station B must acknowledge receipt of message, and as soon as it is ascertained that the whole of the Train has arrived, "Train arrived" is to be sent to station A.

9. Every message affecting the working of the line, such as crossing of trains, &c, is to be copied into the "Line clear message book" before it is despatched, and the receiving station must repeat it to the forwarding station, as a proof of its receipt and correct transmission, and the time of such repetition is to be entered at the foot of both messages. Such messages and repeats are to bear the special prefix, "S.R." (repeated message), which will entitle them to take precedence of all others except "D.G.'s" Stationmasters are, in all cases, to see that these messages are transmitted, and must examine the repetitions with original, to prove their correct transmission.

REGULATIONS FOR WORKING TRAINS WHEN BOTH TELEGRAPHS ARE OUT OF ORDER

10. Should both telegraphs be out of order, no Train shall be permitted to leave until arrangements have been made to work the Line by a Pilotman.

11. When both telegraphs are out of order, the drivers of trains following each other in the same direction must proceed with great caution.

REGULATIONS FOR CROSSING TRAINS AT PLACES WHERE THEY DO NOT USUALLY CROSS EACH OTHER.

12. Trains may only be crossed at places where they do

not usually cross under the following regulations, it being understood that it is never to be done excepting in cases of emergency, or when considerable delay to one of the trains may be avoided thereby, and at none other than the following places, viz:- Hartlebury, Stourport, Bewdley, Bridgnorth, Ironbridge, Buildwas, and Coleham Junction.

13. 1st. It may never be done excepting by direction of the officer in charge of a station.

14. 2ndly. It may never be done unless there be a previous thorough understanding between the officers directing the movements of the respective trains as to what is going to be done. This may be ascertained by means of the Telegraph. Intimation of it should also be communicated to the intermediate stations.

15. 3rdly. Drivers of trains sent on, and also drivers of trains kept back, to cross each other at places where they do not usually cross, are to be furnished with "Crossing orders," directing them to do so, and stating where the trains are to cross, signed by the officers in charge of the respective stations directing the movements of the trains.

16. When the trains are late, and out of their proper course, special arrangements must be made. These are full described in sections 12, 13, 14, and 15. The following is an illustration of them. Suppose two trains have, in an ordinary way, to cross at Bridgnorth, but owing to one being late (say the Down Train), it is arranged by the Bewdley Stationmaster that they shall cross at Bewdley. He telegraphs thus to Bridgnorth:

"Stationmaster, Bewdley, to Stationmaster, Bridgnorth. – No 2 Up Goods Train will cross No. 3 Down Goods at Bewdley"

The message will be entered in the Telegraph Book thus:

Date	*Time*	*From*	*To*
March, 16 1866	2.0pm	Stationmaster, Bewdley	Stationmaster, Bridgnorth

"No 2 Up Goods Train will cross No 3 Down goods at Bewdley, "Repeated—right."

17. The last two words being added after Bridgnorth has received the message and repeated it correctly - Bewdley adding, in acknowledgement, "Right - *see* Section 9, as to the entry of the messages; a crossing order must then be furnished to the engineman and switchman by the Stationmaster at Bridgnorth as the authority for proceeding beyond the usual place for crossing. The Bewdley Stationmaster must also hand his switchman and the driver of the train kept back a copy of the crossing order. The same message must be telegraphed to the intermediate stations, that the stationmasters there may know which train will pass first.

Any defect, in the Instruments, &c, at stations between Shrewsbury and Arley inclusive, must be immediately reported to the Telegraph Lineman at Shrewsbury, and at stations between Bewdley and Hartlebury inclusive, to the Telegraph Lineman at Worcester, and any neglect on his part must be reported to the Telegraph Superintendent at Paddington.

On 30 August 1871 the board authorised the expenditure of £55 for new starting signals at Bewdley and Ironbridge stations; of £22 for 'connecting the down starting signal with the signal box at Buildwas Station', and of £24.15s.0d for 'connecting the starting signal with points at Bridgnorth Station'. Clearly signals were by then being installed to control entry to sections. The 'signal box' at Buildwas was most probably a small cabin covering a ground frame. On 28 February 1872 the board approved the installation of a single needle telegraph instrument at Eardington station, at an estimated cost of £10.6s.3d, no doubt to assist in the safe working of the Forge traffic in the loop siding.

The first mention of interlocking in the district is on 5 February 1873 when the locking of points and signals at Kidderminster was approved at a cost of £169. At this time there were reports of similar work all over the GWR. Saxby's interlocking system had been patented in 1856 and the modern system, whereby one lever movement had to be made before another, first appeared on the LNWR in 1859.

The first mention of such a system on the SVR was on 19 February 1873 when the board approved 'additional signal arrangements and locking of same at Buildwas; £25.'

On the Bewdley - Tenbury - Woofferton line the 'train staff and ticket' system was already in operation by 1872. Under this system no train or engine was allowed onto the single line unless the driver was in possession of the staff, except when another train or engine was to follow in the same direction. The driver would then be shown the staff and issued with a ticket authorising him to enter the section. On arrival at the other end the staff, or ticket, was handed to the signalman. The staffs and tickets were as follows:

Section	Form of staff and ticket	Colour
Woofferton - Tenbury	Triangular	Red
Tenbury - Neen Sollars	Round	Yellow
Neen Sollars - Cleobury Mortimer	Triangular	Blue
Cleobury Mortimer - Bewdley	Square	White

In 1877 preparations were being made for opening the Kidderminster - Bewdley loop. On 29 August the expenditure of £189. 19s. 0d was authorised for block and single-needle telegraph apparatus for the new line and also for completion of the block system between the north and south boxes at Kidderminster, and installing single-needle 'speaking' and double-needle block instruments with switch at the Bewdley Junction. On 24 October the board approved the plan and estimated expenditure of £1,630 for necessary signalling and locking arrangements at Bewdley including the erection of two signal boxes, Bewdley North and South. These were the first proper signal boxes on the SVR. On 4 April 1878 the common seal of the GWR company was ordered to be affixed to an undertaking to the Board of Trade that the loop line would be worked on the train staff and ticket system in conjunction with the block telegraph. The train staff was round and coloured red. A note in the working timetable specified the following whistle code: 'For Severn Valley Line Up and Down, 1 Whistle. To and from Tenbury Line, 2 Whistles. To and from Kidderminster, 3 Whistles. Kidderminster Junction: - Main Line, Up and Down, 1 Whistle. To and from Branch Line, 2 Whistles.' The loop opened on 1 June 1878.

It will be recalled from chapter 5 that Col Rich had required alterations at the junction at Bewdley. Because of this, according to a report to the board on 9 January 1879, an additional expenditure of £618.9s.5d had been incurred above the authorised £1,630 in the signalling and locking of the station and junction. The entire work was carried out by McKenzie & Holland. Their account also included an additional £126. 6s. 6d for gas fittings at the station. The signal boxes were of standard McKenzie & Holland pattern.

During 1880 the GWR carried out a detailed survey of the SVR as part of its survey of the entire system. The plan, to a scale of 2 chains to 1 inch, shows the route in great detail and shows exactly what was there at that time.[2] All the signal boxes, other than Bewdley, date from after 1880. Some indication of the approximate dates of their installation can be gained from the minutes of the GWR Board and Traffic Committee, though there are few direct references to signal boxes. On 18 October 1882 tenders were accepted from McKenzie & Holland for locking at Highley (£315), Hampton Loade (£315) and Arley (£300). These prices probably included the signal boxes which were certainly erected around this time. Additional platforms were built at Arley and Hampton Loade and the completed works were inspected by Col Rich and were given BoT sanction on 25 June 1883.[3]

At Stourport the new canal basin created more shunting movements and to meet BoT requirements an expenditure of £1,346 10s. 0d was authorised on 4 June 1885 for rearranging and interlocking the points and signals in the station yard. Two signal boxes were erected, the North containing eighteen working levers and six spares by the level crossing and the South near the canal bridge containing fourteen working levers and four spares. Col Rich's report on his inspection of the new works, dated 13 January 1886, sanctioned their use subject to a few requirements.[4] On 5 October 1887 the board approved the expenditure of £13. 4s. 6d to establish double-line block working between Stourport North and South boxes.

Bewdley was again the scene of a collision, on 10 October 1888, when the 18.55 passenger train from Shrewsbury ran past the home signal which was at danger and collided with the 18.30 goods from Tenbury. Robert Wright, the driver of the passenger train, attended the board and admitted negligence. He was suspended without pay for two weeks and lost twenty days towards his next bonus, but in view of his length of service and good conduct he was allowed to resume duty.

Buildwas, the other junction station besides Bewdley, was next to receive attention. On 4 February 1886 the board ordered the block telegraph to be installed between Buildwas and Much Wenlock, and on 10 March the expenditure of £67. 6s. 2d was authorised. Further signalling work, authorised on 16 November 1887 at an estimated cost of £2,080, included renewal of locking apparatus and signals and completing the block telegraph. Two signal boxes, erected about that time, were no doubt included in the cost which, it was reported in the Engineering Committee minutes on 16 January 1889, exceeded the authorised amount by £156. 7s. 10d.

In his report on the new works at Arley, Highley and Hampton Loade, 23 June 1883,[3] Col Rich remarked: 'This railway is a single line and I regret to report that it is worked by telegraph.' This working continued for another eight years. The GWR service timetable for January 1892 revealed that at last, on 25 October 1891, train staff and ticket working, in conjunction with the single-needle block telegraph, was introduced between Hartlebury and Sutton Bridge Junction. The staffs and tickets were as follows:

Hartlebury Junction - Stourport	square	red
Stourport - Bewdley (South)	triangular	green
Bewdley North - Arley	hexagonal	yellow
Arley - Hampton Loade	square	red

Hampton Loade - Bridgnorth	triangular	green
Bridgnorth - Ironbridge	hexagonal	yellow
Ironbridge - Buildwas	square	red
Buildwas - Sutton Bridge Junction	triangular	green

It will be seen that only three types of staff were used and that Highley, Coalport, Cressage and Berrington were not staff stations, and trains could not be crossed there.

At Bridgnorth in 1891-2 two new signal boxes were erected, one south of the station on the 'up' side beyond the bridge over the approach road to the goods yard; and one north of the station, on the 'down' side near where the tracks converged into single line. The estimated cost of £3,013 was approved on 13 August 1891, and the signal boxes were opened in October 1892.

On 12 April 1893 the board authorised a large programme of works on the Severn Valley branch at an estimated cost of £9,542. Most important was the installation of the electric train staff (introduced on the GWR in 1891) over the entire length of the line, from Hartlebury Junction to Sutton Bridge Junction, £2,154, including the 'back road' at Bewdley; and from Kidderminster to Bewdley and Tenbury, £500.

In conjunction with this, three new signal boxes were opened in 1894: Ironbridge where the total expenditure was about £1,545; Cressage where an additional platform was built (see chapter 6) to make the station a crossing place, £2,435; and the same at Berrington, £1,838. At Cressage the signal box contained nineteen working levers, four spares and a gate wheel for the level crossing, and there was a two-lever ground frame, locked from the signal box, to work the loop points and FPL at the north end of the station. Berrington signal box had sixteen working and three spare levers and here also there was a two-lever ground frame, locked from the signal box, to work the loop points at the south end of the station.[5] Electric staff working came into operation in January 1894 between Hartlebury Junction and Buildwas Junction. From there to Sutton Bridge Junction staff and ticket working remained in operation. Highley became a staff station, and electric train staff working was introduced also between Bewdley South and North boxes through the 'back road' only.

To avoid congestion at Shrewsbury, it was made possible for a train to be held on the Severn Valley line at Sutton Bridge while another train entered the line. The loop from just north of the 'Potts' bridge at 39 miles 53 chains to Sutton Bridge Junction, a length of 18 chains, was made into a double-track section. At the south end of the loop on the down side a signal box with ten levers, named Burnt Mill Junction, was opened on 1 January 1894. Electric train staff working was now extended from Buildwas to Cressage, Berrington and Burnt Mill Junction. The double line section from here to Sutton Bridge Junction, and also those between the south and north boxes at Stourport, Bewdley, Bridgnorth and Buildwas Junction, were worked by double-line disc block telegraph.

Coalport was the last station to be made into a crossing place, during 1894-5. Besides the new down platform, a signal box was erected south of the station and a two-lever ground frame, locked from the signal box, was installed at the north end to operate the points and FPL there. The signal box had twenty-four working levers and seven spares. The reason for the extra ground frames here and at Cressage and Berrington was that the distance of the points from the signal box was regarded as too great for a run of rodding. About 1930 these points were motorised and the ground frames were removed. Signalling and interlocking works were passed by Col Yorke for the BoT on 7 January 1896.[6]

Despite improvements in signalling and interlocking, ultimate safety still depended upon human discipline, as was shown by a derailment at Arley on 29 November 1898. The driver of the 15.10 passenger train from Hartlebury failed to stop at the down home signal which was at danger and the train ran through just as the signalman was changing the points for the loop. Presumably locking bars had not yet been installed. Driver and fireman were suspended for a week without pay. It seems strange now that the signalmen should have been allowed to accept a passenger train from Bewdley before setting and locking the points for the loop.

To facilitate permanent way and other maintenance work along the line, the provision of telephones and occupation key instruments was approved on 22 November 1906, at a cost of £760. These were installed in cabins along the line. By removing the occupation key from the instrument, with the co-operation of the signalmen at each end of the section, the gangers or other workers on the line could ensure that no train or engine would enter the section while work was in progress. The mechanical trolleys for the gangers were obtained from W.A. Green at a total cost of £112. 10s. 0d included in the above sum.

The renewal of the interlocking frame and point and signal connections at Buildwas was authorised on 12 April 1905 at a cost of £692 and the same at Bewdley South on 19 March 1909, at £750. At Hartlebury Junction the interlocking frame, installed when the box was opened in 1880, was reported to be worn out and its renewal was authorised in October 1909 at a cost of £740, increased by £93 one year later. The frame was renewed in 1912. It is greatly to be hoped that the SVR interlocking frames will give longer service than thirty-two years. The renewal cost of £833 in 1910 is equivalent to about £25,000 in the late 1980s.

To expedite the handling of the increased coal traffic, brought about by the construction during 1913 of the railway from New Billingsley colliery, a new goods loop was opened and a signal box was built at the junction and named 'Kinlet and Billingsley Sidings', with thirty-two working levers and six spares. It was inspected by Col Yorke whose report recommending sanction by the BoT is dated 28 April.[7] The box was open from 08.00 to 16.00 and was the only one on the Severn Valley line which could be switched out. The short sections, Arley - Kinlet and Kinlet - Highley were worked with electric train staff, but the long section, Arley - Highley, was worked by electric tablet, presumably Tyers No 7. This section has thus been worked by five different systems: single-needle telegraph, train staff and ticket, electric staff, electric tablet, and now by electric token.

At Iron Bridge & Broseley the interlocking frame, level crossing gates and gearing, point and signal connections were renewed in 1916. The estimated expenditure of £1,050 was approved on 13 January. By way of simplifying operations at Buildwas and Bridgnorth the north and south signal boxes were replaced in 1922-3 by a central signal box at each place. Excess expenditure of £488 on the Bridgnorth box was approved on 2 August 1923. This box, closed on 2 December 1963, was demolished just before the present SVR took over. It was regrettably rebuilt in the same place. The site of the former south box would have proved a better position for operating the present terminal layout, but the cost of erecting a new box here would have been beyond the means of the SVR Society. Buildwas central box, opened in November 1923, with 113 levers, was the largest on the line. The more remote points were motorised.

Burnt Mill Junction box was closed on 14 February 1937 and the points there were motorised and operated from Sutton Bridge Junction. An auxiliary staff instrument was installed in a cabin by the points, to enable the driver of an up train held in the loop to obtain a staff released from Sutton Bridge Junction box, following arrival of a down train.

Although the electric token apparatus had been installed by the GWR on the Great Marlow branch as early as January 1914, the Severn Valley had to wait until after World War II before it was installed. By 1950 electric token working was in use through all the sections except Bridgnorth - Coalport - Iron Bridge and Buildwas - Cressage - Berrington. The double-line sections Stourport South - North and Bewdley South - North were worked by double-line disc block telegraph. Despite the recommendations of Col Pringle after the inquiry into the Abermule disaster of January 1921, the token instruments at Arley and Hampton Loade were in the station booking offices and the electric staff instrument at Buildwas was in a cabin on the station platform. The Arley and Hampton

Loade instruments were transferred to the signal boxes by the present SVR.

At Stourport signalling and point connections were re-arranged in 1951, the north signal box and frame were extended and the south box was closed on 1 April and removed. Bewdley North signal box was raised bodily by about a foot in 1954 to give greater space beneath the lever frame. Various changes were made in the layout and signalling at Bewdley when the SVR took over since its function as a junction station in both directions no longer existed. Points were removed at the north end of the station because it was unnecessary for trains at platform 3 to run to and form the Tenbury line. The up and down lines through platforms 2 and 1 respectively became the only stretch of double-line on a British 'preserved' railway. The line through platform 3 is signalled for both directions. Latterly on BR it was worked by electric train tokens between the South and North boxes, but this system was replaced on the SVR by track circuits and a direction lever in each box. The lever is pulled back to let a train in; this locks the direction lever in the other box and unlocks the appropriate signal levers.

LOCOMOTIVES

The operating company at the opening of the SVR in 1862 was the West Midland whose locomotive superintendent at that time was Edward Wilson. He remained in charge until the WMR was absorbed by the GWR in 1863, when for a short time he took charge of the entire standard gauge locomotive department at Wolverhampton. This was the period when George Armstrong was taking over command at Wolverhampton from his elder brother Joseph, who succeeded Daniel Gooch at Swindon. The West Midland locomotive stock at the amalgamation on 1 August 1863 totalled 131 by various makers, comprising sixty-five six-coupled goods tender engines, thirty-five four-coupled passenger tender engines, fifteen tender singles and sixteen tanks. In the absence of positive records it is not possible to state which types worked on the SVR, but one type is mentioned,[8] the four double-framed 2–4–0s, WM Nos 93–6, GWR 190–3, built by E.B. Wilson & Co in 1855-6. These 5ft 6in engines, similar to the OWW 21 class (GWR 182 class), were twice rebuilt by the GWR at Wolverhampton and were withdrawn in 1899-1903. They were stationed at Worcester which, with Coleham at Shrewsbury, provided the SVR motive power.

Another OWW type known to have worked on the SVR was the GWR 171 class double-framed 2–4–0. A photograph of No 180 of this class (R. & W. Hawthorn No 829 of 1853) on Wribbenhall viaduct in 1897 is shown on p68. This engine, OWW No 16, was rebuilt at Wolverhampton in May 1875 and March 1891 and was taken out of stock in June 1898. Another photograph (p68) shows Armstrong 2–4–0T No 1A with the inspector's special train standing on the Dowles bridge over the Severn near Bewdley on the Tenbury line on 5 August 1864. This engine was built at Wolverhampton in 1864, renumbered 17 in 1865, rebuilt to saddle tank 1867 and withdrawn 1889.

Other classes known from photographic evidence to have worked on the SVR were the Joseph Armstrong 'Standard Goods' double-framed 0–6–0, 388 class, built at Swindon 1866-76; and his 927 class 0–6–0s or 'Coal Engines', built at Swindon in 1874, also with double frames. Passenger trains were worked by the 439 class 6ft 1in 2–4–0s with inside frames built under George Armstrong at Wolverhampton in 1885-6. These were replacements of Joseph Armstrong's 439 class known as the 'bicycles' because of their exposed wheels. Another Joseph Armstrong class which worked on the Severn Valley trains was the 2–4–0 'Metro Tank' with inside frames, built at Swindon from 1869 to 1899, the last batches under Dean who took over in 1877. The 2021 class 6ft 6$^{1}/_{2}$in inside-framed 2–4–0s, which also worked many of the passenger trains, were built at Swindon under Dean in 1881-2. They were a domeless-boilered development of the Joseph Armstrong 806 class of 1873.

The completion of the Bewdley - Kidderminster loop in 1878 brought a further demand for locomotives. A report in *The Kidderminster Shuttle*, Saturday 23 March 1878, stated that 'The new engines for the loop line are all ready at Wolverhampton.' No 'new engines' of a suitable type were completed in 1877 or early 1878. The last of the 'standard goods' was completed by the GWR in October 1876. The report probably referred to 'newly repaired' engines.

Soon after this Dean's engines began to appear. The most numerous, frequently to be seen on the SVR for around sixty years, were the 2301 or 'Dean Goods' 0–6–0 type, built at Swindon from 1883 to 1899. Some of the smaller Dean 4–4–0s such as the 'Dukes' were also seen from time to time.

From about the middle of 1919 the GWR introduced the 'route colour' system denoting the maximum axle load. Locomotives carried a coloured circle on the cab side. On the SVR, 'yellow' engines, with a maximum axle load of 16 tons, were unrestricted; 'bluc' cngines, up to 17 tons 12cwt, were restricted to a maximum speed of 25mph, but 2–8–0s, with a maximum axle load of 17 tons 5cwt, were excluded, for what reason is not clear. There may have been clearance problems. The 2–6–2 tanks, 51xx and 81xx were restricted to 25mph between Victoria Bridge and Linley. Hartlebury - Bewdley was classified 'dotted red' indicating that engines with an axle load over 17 tons 12cwt (excluding 'Kings' and 47xx 2–8–0s) were permitted subject to a maximum speed of 20mph. Similar engines were allowed between Buildwas and Shrewsbury, but on running lines only.

Locomotives worked mainly from the sheds at Stourbridge, Worcester and Shrewsbury. There was a small shed near Kidderminster station housing two engines which occasionally worked the SVR or Tenbury line. On 1 February 1932 a new shed at Kidderminster came into use and the old one was closed. The new shed was on the south side of the loop line to Bewdley just west of the bridge under Hoo Road. It was built under the Loans and Guarantees Act of 1929. Preparation of the site involved the removal of 10,000 tons of sand which was sent to the GWR works at Swindon, Wolverhampton and Caerphilly. The shed was originally built in 1921 at Brassaleg on the Brecon & Merthyr Railway near Newport.

It was a steel-framed structure, measuring 200ft x 30ft, clad in 'corrugated iron', and it contained two roads. On the north side was a row of offices built in brick. The coal stage was the usual GWR type, with a 26,000 gallon water tank on top. There was no turntable in the layout, although there was one at the old shed, but this was cut up some time after the shed was demolished about March 1934. At the end of 1947 there were sixteen locomotives stationed at Kidderminster: 2–6–0 5303; small 2–6–2Ts 4584, 4586, 4594, 5518, 5573; large 2–6–2Ts 4153, 5110, 8101; and 0–6–0PTs 28 and 29 (ex Cleobury Mortimer & Ditton Priors Light Railway); 2093; 4625, 7700, 8718, 8727. The new shed was closed on 10 August 1964.

In its last years, passenger trains in the section between Shrewsbury and Bridgnorth were frequently worked by former LMS 'Fowler' 2–6–4Ts and Stanier 2–6–2Ts. In 1957 three BR standard Class 3 2–6–2Ts worked the trains. On the Tenbury line GWR diesel railcars took some of the turns.

TRAIN SERVICES

As can be seen from the timetable for February 1862 (p53), the passenger service at the opening was somewhat sparse, consisting of three through trains each way taking from 2h 3min to 2h 15min, at an average speed of under 20mph, and a train from Bridgnorth to Shrewsbury in the morning and back in the evening, with no Sunday service. By 1869 there were four through trains each way and one on Sundays, and the best time had come down to 1h 39min, Hartlebury - Shrewsbury. Between Bewdley and Woofferton there were three trains each way on weekdays only. The same pattern continued for several years. The public was not satisfied with the service as is proved by references in the board minutes to 'memorials' from inhabitants of Stourport, Bewdley and Bridgnorth requesting a better service, generally followed by 'This cannot be acceded to at present.'

The timetable for February 1876 showed four through passenger trains each way and one each way on Sundays. Two of the weekday trains and the Sunday trains ran to and from Worcester. The fastest time between Hartlebury and Shrewsbury was still 1h 55min. The Sunday service, being the only train on the line, was operated 'one engine in steam'. The working timetable for May 1872 showed only a sparse service on the Bewdley - Woofferton line. There were three through trains, to Bewdley, and two down plus one involving a wait of 1h 40min at Tenbury. In addition, there were two each way Tenbury and Woofferton (spelt Wooferton).

By February 1878, after years of delay, the Kidderminster - Bewdley loop was approaching completion, and both the GWR and LNWR were directing their attention to its future use. Mr. P.H. Munty, the standing arbitrator between the two companies, submitted an award to the GWR board on 6 February on the service to be operated for the LNWR over the Tenbury - Bewdley line. The GWR was to run a daily train, except Sundays, from Snow Hill, Birmingham, about 9.00 and another about 16.15 to take up traffic at Smethwick Junction (now Smethwick West) and also to run a daily train from Newport (Mon) at or about 8.00 to take up the traffic from Tenbury. This arrangement was to remain in force for five years, unless the two parties agreed upon a change. A draft timetable of trains on the loop was submitted on 20 February.

On 22 May 1878, following a request from the Mayor and residents of Bridgnorth for improved connections to Birmingham and London, it was agreed, as an experiment, to make some improvements to the service as recommended by the general manager. A train was put on leaving Bridgnorth at 9.00, Bewdley at 9.22 and arriving at Worcester at 9.55 to connect with the 10.00 to Paddington arriving there at 15.30. But there was no comparable return service, and the fast train was apparently not a great success because it was withdrawn after a few years.

From the opening of the SVR, trains shuttled up and down between Buildwas and Much Wenlock connecting with the through SVR trains. With the connection to Coalbrookdale and Lightmoor open from 1 November 1864 the service was extended to Wellington and, from 16 December 1867, to Craven Arms. The timetable for June 1880 showed two through passenger trains and one mixed train each way on weekdays only, and one each way between Much Wenlock and Wellington on Sundays.

Following the opening of the Kidderminster - Bewdley line a service of four through passenger trains was operated between Kidderminster and Woofferton and beyond. Using running powers granted in an agreement of 1863, the LNWR ran a coal train daily leaving Leominster at 15.40 and arriving at Kidderminster at 21.30. A corresponding LNWR empties left Kidderminster at 15.00 and arrived at Leominster at 19.30. Other LNWR traffic may have run as required but it is not shown in the working timetable. The LNWR also ran through passenger coaches between Birmingham New Street and Woofferton. These were attached at Smethwick Junction to the back of GWR trains running from Snow Hill, and vice versa. The LNWR goods trains had disappeared from the working timetables by 1903 and the through passenger coaches were discontinued from 1 January 1917. It was curious that with the opening of the Kidderminster loop 'up' and 'down' directions on the Tenbury line were reversed and Kidderminster to Woofferton became 'up', so that 'down' or 'up' trains passed through Bewdley in opposite directions. The more logical description was later restored.

Train services between Bewdley and Kidderminster were not entirely satisfactory at first. A letter in *The Kidderminster Times*, 11 April 1885, commented on the poor facilities for persons going to Bewdley for recreation on the river. They had to leave Bewdley at 20.32 to return to Kidderminster via Hartlebury, arriving at 21.20. There was need for a train about 21.15 to connect with the 21.29 to Stourbridge. In a note at the end the editor added: 'The train service on the Bewdley loop line has long called for revision and improvement.' In the 1880s there were still four through trains each way between Hartlebury and Shrewsbury and one on Sundays, but the overall times had not improved; the best was 1h 45min and the worst 2h 14min.

It will be recalled from chapter 6 that in early March 1885 the rail interchange basin on the canal at Stourport came into use. On 7 March the following announcement appeared in *The Kidderminster Shuttle*:

> **STOURPORT** HEAVY CLAIM BY THE GREAT WESTERN RAILWAY COMPANY AGAINST THE LONDON & NORTH WESTERN RAILWAY COMPANY
> We understand that, at the present time, there is being heard *in camera* a claim for a very large amount against the London & North Western Railway by the directors of the Great Western Railway with regard to transport of goods from Stourport and other districts over which the Shropshire Union Canal Carrying Company has supervision. The trial is of much public interest just now, seeing that the various railway companies are endeavouring to obtain parliamentary powers for increasing their maximum rates and enforcing terminal charges. As is well known the Great Western Railway is supreme along the whole Severn Valley from Worcester to Shrewsbury, there being no other competing railway (except at Coalport LNWR. JM) and the only kind of opposition is the Shropshire Union Canal Carrying Company. The railway rates in the district are felt to be so high that the greater portion of the goods sent from this and other districts similarly situated go by canal. Now the contention of the Great Western Railway Company is that the canal is now in the hands of the London & North Western Railway Company, and that according to certain agreements this company has no power to compete with the Great Western Railway as carriers by water. A sum between £40,000 and £50,000 is said to be claimed by the plaintiffs as compensation. Several witnesses from this district have been in London during the week for the purpose of giving evidence upon the trial.

The outcome has not been discovered. The Shropshire Union did in fact have a warehouse at Kidderminster and operated its boats through to Stourport. The warehouse remained, lettered 'London, Midland & Scottish Railway Boatage Depot', until its demolition in 1973. But the Staffordshire & Worcestershire Canal was never 'in the hands of the LNWR'; it remained independent until nationalisation.

On the Tenbury line at this time (1887) there were four trains each way weekdays only between Kidderminster and Woofferton, $24^1/_4$ miles, in 1h 10min. The single fare was 4s 0d third class and 8s 6d first class, expensive for 1887. The same journey, made by the author in 1959, cost 3s 6d return. On 16 December 1896, on the recommendation of the general manager, the board approved the running of a train at 8.40 from Kidderminster to Bewdley and Woofferton on Tuesdays, 'the additional mileage involved being 48 per week.' This suggests a balancing service, but it is not clear from the timetables which this was. The train evidently satisfied a demand because it became a daily service, arriving at Woofferton at 9.55.

In 1904 the number of trains on the SVR had increased to six through each way on weekdays, plus one each way between Bridgnorth and Hartlebury, and one to and from Bridgnorth and one to and from Shrewsbury on Sundays. Two to Shrewsbury were through from Worcester and there was one return to Worcester. But the trains were still slow; the fastest took 1h 45min, an average speed of under 23mph, for the 41 miles between Hartlebury and Shrewsbury. On the Tenbury line there were five each way between Kidderminster and Woofferton. The journey time for the 24 miles varied from 1h 12min to 1h 42min. A similar pattern of services continued through World War I.

The opening of the Kidderminster - Stourport Electric Tramway in April 1898 was mentioned in chapter 6. On 7 October 1898 it was reported to the GWR board that the tramway had caused electrical troubles with the Block system at Kidderminster and Stourport, and it had been necessary to use specially insulated sections between Churchill (Blakedown) and Hartlebury North (Junction), Kidderminster South and Bewdley South, and Bewdley South and Stourport South boxes, at the three points where the tramway crossed the GWR. The cost, £44, was paid by the British Electric Traction Co Ltd, contractors for the tramway. In May 1900 another scheme was put forward for a tramway, or 'light railway' along the road from Kidderminster to Bewdley, engineered by Stephen Sellon. No Act was obtained and nothing more was heard of the scheme.

Local train services all over the country were being threatened by electric trams at this period. Several railway companies, including the GWR, responded by introducing steam rail-motors consisting of a coach and a small four-wheeled locomotive, either incorporated within it or as a separate unit to which the coach was articulated. The GWR rail-motors, introduced in 1903 on the Chalford - Stonehouse service, had an engine unit forming a bogie at one end of the coach. On Thursday, 29 December 1904 one of these was tried on the Kidderminster - Bewdley - Stourport section, with apparent success, because on Monday, 2 January 1905 a full service was inaugurated.[10] Foley Park Halt, on the Bewdley - Kidderminster loop, was opened on the same day. Rifle Range Halt, on the Bewdley side of the tunnel, near the Devil's Spittleful, was opened in June 1905. Two rail-motors operated a fairly frequent service, a typical run being Kidderminster dep 7.15, Bewdley 7.25, dep 7.28, Stourport 7,35, dep 7.40, Bewdley 7.47 dep 7.50, Kidderminster 8.00. On 15 December 1910 the general manager recommended the running of an additional rail-motor on the Hartlebury - Stourport - Bewdley section, to start on 2 January 1911. The rail-motors operated until 1918.[11] Rifle Range Halt was closed on 4 October 1920 but Foley Park Halt lasted until withdrawal of the BR passenger service in 1970.

Another light railway of a different sort, projected in 1900, actually contributed traffic to the GWR. This was the Cleobury Mortimer & Ditton Priors Light Railway, laid out by E.R. Calthrop of Leek and Manifold Valley fame. This, however, was a standard-gauge line leaving the Bewdley - Tenbury line by a south-facing junction at Cleobury Mortimer station and following the valley of the River Rea to Ditton Priors. Its purpose was to serve farming communities along the valley and to provide a railhead for the dhustone quarry being opened up on Brown Clee Hill to which it was connected by a cable-worked incline. Its total length was 12 miles 67ch. Track consisted of 72 lb flat bottomed rails bolted through sole plates to wooden sleepers. Goods traffic began on 19 July 1908; a passenger service was operated from 20 November using ex North London Railway four-wheeled coaches. Under the Railways Act of 1921 the railway was absorbed by the GWR on 1 January 1923. The old CM&DP rolling stock was replaced by slightly less ancient GWR stock and the passenger service continued to run until 24 September 1938. By then stone traffic from the Abdon quarry had also ended. With the imminence of World War II the line became used as an ammunition store. Dumps appeared along the line and a large depot was established at Ditton Priors. After the war remaining ammunition was removed and on 1 January 1948 the line passed to the Western Region of BR. On 1 May 1957 it was taken over by the Admiralty who established a depot at Ditton Priors which they operated until 1965.[12]

In 1919 the working timetables showed the miners' trains to and from Highley, four each way. The pattern of services on the Bridgnorth and Tenbury lines changed. Some SVR trains ran through between Worcester or Hartlebury and Shrewsbury, others ran from Kidderminster to Shrewsbury. Passengers from Worcester changed to a connecting rail-motor service at Hartlebury, and vice versa. The Rail-motors shuttled to and fro between Kidderminster, Bewdley, Stourport and Hartlebury complementing the services on the Bridgnorth and Tenbury lines. There were no Sunday services.

There was little change following the grouping on 1 January 1923 which hardly affected the GWR in England. Overall times were practically the same as in the 1870s, for example the 7.00 from Worcester left Hartlebury at 7.28 and arrived at

Scene at Bridgnorth on re-opening day, 23 May 1970. Ivatt 2–6–0 No 43106 and Stanier 8F 2–8–0 No 8233 (Peter E. Baughan)

WD 2–10–0 No 600 *Gordon*, formerly on Longmoor Military Railway, leaving Bridgnorth for Hampton Loade on 22 April 1973 (John Marshall)

0–6–0 pannier tank No 5764 and German 2–6–2T No 064 305–6 at Bridgnorth on 27 September 1975 (John Marshall)

Bridgnorth yard and shed, 30 August 1981. The two Western diesel-hydraulics can be seen behind the platform (John Marshall)

Work in progress on the bridge over Bridgnorth by-pass, 3 January 1983 (John Marshall)

2–6–4T No 80079 on the first train out of Bridgnorth to cross the by-pass bridge, on 5 March 1983 (John Marshall)

'King Arthur' class 4–6–0 No 777 *Sir Lamiel*, on loan from the NRM, at Bridgnorth on the 14.30 to Bewdley, 30 April 1983, one of the last trains out before the embankment collapse (John Marshall)

The collapsed embankment just south of the Bridgnorth by-pass bridge on 2 May 1983 (John Marshall)

Class 5 4–6–0 No 5000, from the National Collection, leaving Bridgnorth on the 12.15 to Bewdley, crossing the by-pass bridge and the newly restored embankment on 1 September 1983 (John Marshall)

Work in progress on the new Kidderminster Town (SVR) station, 3 May 1984 (John Marshall)

D1013 *Western Ranger* on the first SVR train into Kidderminster, by permission of BR, with the 6 ton steam crane for track laying, 11 May 1984 (John Marshall)

Opening day at Kidderminster Town station, 30 July 1984. 4930 *Hagley Hall* backing onto the VIP special (John Marshall)

Kidderminster Town station with 2–6–2T No 4566 in the platform, 7 April 1988 (John Marshall)

The frontage of Kidderminster Town station, modelled on Ross on Wye station, 27 March 1988. An awning is still to be fitted in front and ornamental iron crestings on the flat roofs. (John Marshall)

Kidderminster station signal box, 7 April 1988 (John Marshall)

The SVR signal gantry at Kidderminster, 7 April 1988 (John Marshall)

Bewdley by-pass bridge works on 19 July 1986; 2–8–0 No 8233 passing with a train from Kidderminster (John Marshall)

Bewdley by-pass bridge from the south, 10.50 on 6 November, at the moment of completion of sliding it into place from the pad in the foreground (John Marshall)

Reconstructing the embankment at Bewdley by-pass bridge, 23 November 1986 (John Marshall)

One of the first trains over Bewdley by-pass bridge, 30 November 1986, headed by 2–6–2T No 4566 (John Marshall)

Diesel train from Birmingham entering Bewdley on the 'Enthusiasts' Day' on 10 September 1983 (John Marshall)

LMS 0–6–0T No 47383 at Bewdley with the demonstration goods train on the same day (John Marshall)

BR Class 4 4–6–0 No 75069 nearing the end of its overhaul in the workshop at Bridgnorth, 26 August 1983 (John Marshall)

LNWR Webb 0–6–2 'Coal Tank' No 1054, on loan from Dinting Railway Centre, at Highley on 5 October 1986 (John Marshall)

GWR 4–4–0 No 3440 *City of Truro*, on loan from the NRM, at Bewdley on 11 June 1986 after its complete overhaul at Bridgnorth and repainting at Bewdley (John Marshall)

The ex GWR hand crane ADW 446 on the Stourport siding at Bewdley, 28 June 1985 (John Marshall)

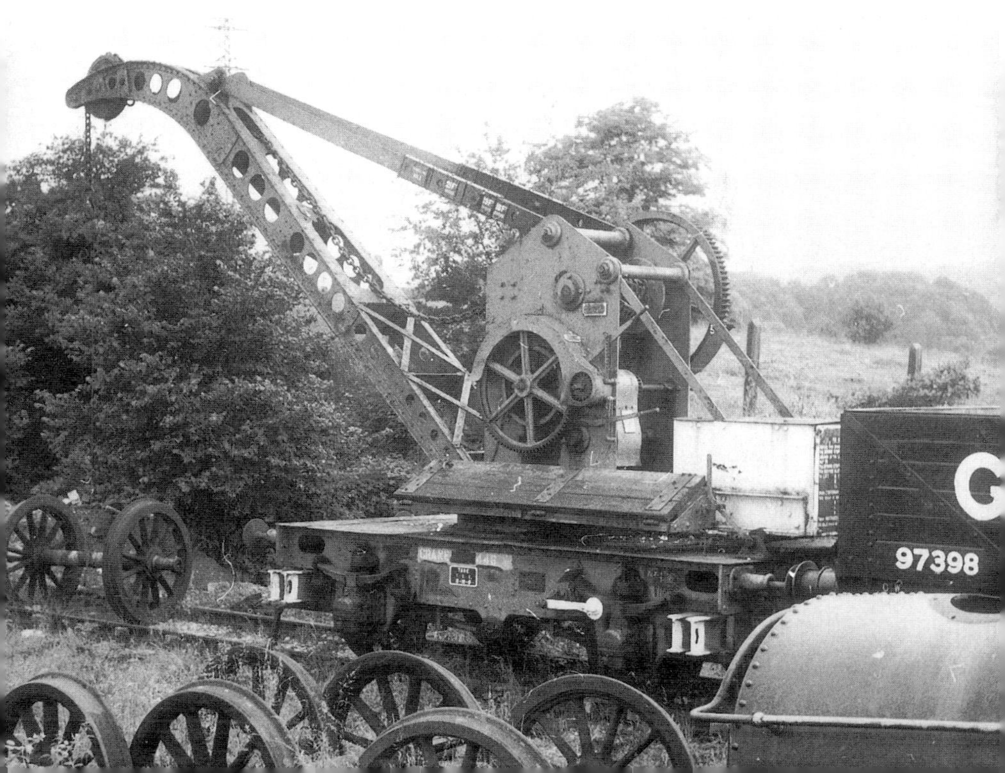

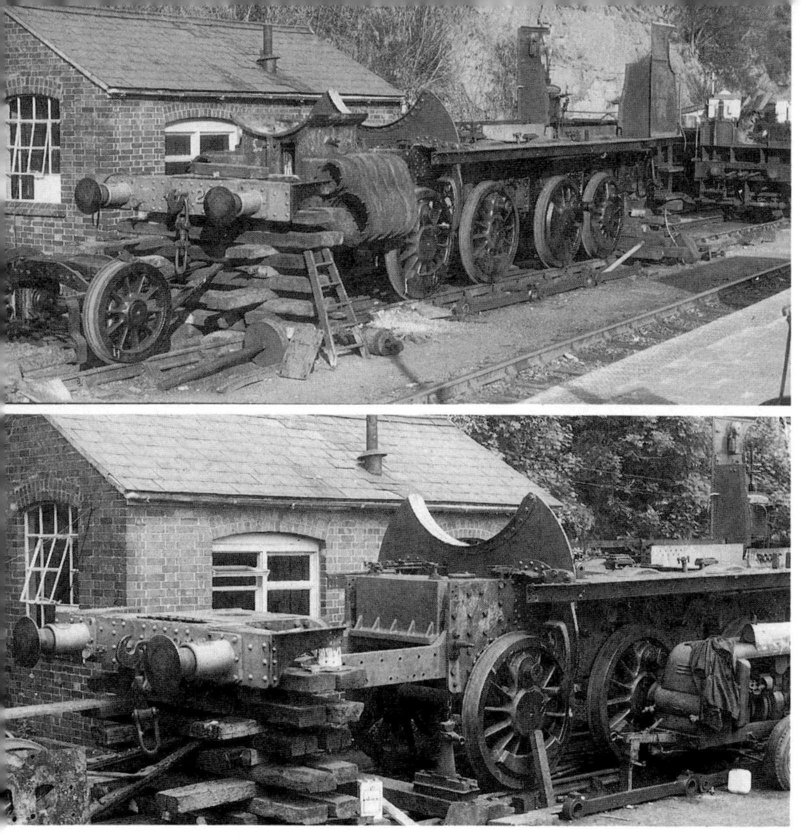

(*above*) GWR 2–8–0 No 2857, dismantled at Bewdley, on 11 April 1982. The old cracked cylinder block is about to be removed to be replaced by a better one, a long and massive operation. (John Marshall)

(*centre*) Frames of 2857 after removal of old cylinder block, 19 June 1982 (John Marshall)

(*below*) On 5 May 1985, with new cylinders in place and boiler refitted, 2857 nears completion of its restoration (John Marshall)

2857 entering Bewdley on a train from Bridgnorth, 7 September 1986 (John Marshall)

A fine piece of work by the Carriage & Wagon Department at Bewdley. Invalid carriage 9055 on 29 August 1985, rebuilt from a GWR saloon of 1912 (John Marshall)

Kidderminster carriage & wagon workshop, 7 April 1988. The BR station is on the right (John Marshall)

Rebuilt 'West Country' class 4–6–2 No 34027 *Taw Valley*, still unpainted after recent overhaul at Bridgnorth, on test on a train at Bewdley by the North signal box, 27 October 1987 (John Marshall)

Shrewsbury at 9.25. A train ran from Hartlebury to Shrewsbury on Sunday mornings and back in the evenings, May to October. All through the 1920s and '30s the trains jogged to and fro on the same general timings.

On the evening of Friday, 13 January 1928 the 19.45 ex Shrewsbury, three coaches behind small 2–6–2T 5508, was passing Bridgnorth Golf Club, north of Bridgnorth tunnel, when it left the rails. About 250 yards of track was torn up. No-one was injured, though the fact that there were only four passengers on the train is an indication of the usage of SVR services even in the 1920s. Breakdown gangs from Shrewsbury and Worcester had the line restored by 17.30 the following day. Mr C.B. Collett, CME of the GWR, visited the scene from Swindon. No fault was found on the locomotive which was less than a year old and had travelled only 8,492 miles. The cause of the accident was attributed to several rotten sleepers which had allowed the rails to spread.[13]

In summer 1930 there were six trains each way between Kidderminster, Bewdley and Tenbury and nine between Tenbury and Woofferton. Frequently through passengers had to change at Tenbury. A similar inconvenience was often found at Bridgnorth. Bewdley saw the most trains, with its locals as well as the Tenbury and Bridgnorth trains, with over sixty arrivals and departures daily. Even during the second world war there were five weekday trains each way between Bewdley and Shrewsbury with through connections to and from Hartlebury and Kidderminster, and four each way between Kidderminster and Woofferton with extras between Woofferton and Tenbury. The SVR was exceedingly busy at this time, handling a vast amount of freight traffic and troop trains. A large RAF camp near Bridgnorth brought a good deal of traffic.

After the war a decline set in. The miners' trains continued to and from Highley, but in 1947 there was only one through train from Shrewsbury to Hartlebury and three from Hartlebury to Shrewsbury. Other journeys required a change, at Bewdley, Bridgnorth or Ironbridge. There were five through services each way on the Tenbury line, of which three were diesel railcars. On 1 January 1948 the SVR from Hartlebury to Shrewsbury, the connecting lines from Kidderminster to Bewdley and Woofferton, and Wellington to Buildwas, Much Wenlock and Craven Arms, became part of the Western Region of BR. Apart from minor alterations, the pattern of services remained the same between Shrewsbury and Hartlebury or Kidderminster for the next fourteen years. On the Wenlock line between Much Wenlock and Craven Arms, traffic was so light that from 31 December 1951 the passenger service was withdrawn and the line from Longville to Marsh Farm Junction was closed entirely, but an infrequent goods service was maintained from Longville to Much Wenlock. Iron Bridge & Broseley signal box was closed on 25 November 1956 and Maw's Siding signal box on 18 October 1959. Other services managed to struggle on into the 1960s but, despite the economies brought about by the use of the GWR diesel railcars, there was insufficient traffic to keep the lines open. With Beeching in control, under direction to bring about a viable railway network, all loss-making lines were doomed.

Next to succumb was the Woofferton - Tenbury section, closed to passengers on 31 July 1961. The Tenbury - Bewdley passenger service lingered on until 1 August 1962, and the Much Wenlock - Buildwas - Wellington until 23 July 1962. Severn Valley services, too, were under threat. Although token attempts at economy had been made by the use of GWR and BR single-unit railcars, more could have been done by converting the lesser-used stations into unstaffed halts. The passenger timetables could have been made more convenient and the scenic attractions of the route advertised, but even these measures could not have saved the railway. In common with other rural railways, there was little hope for freight traffic, and with the running down of the Wyre Forest collieries there was almost nothing left. The Ironbridge Gorge, once the cradle of the Industrial Revolution, was now little more than material for the future museum complex, a haven for the industrial archaeologist. Modern industrial concerns, requiring more space and better access than such a site could offer, developed elsewhere. The entire valley could not offer enough traffic to keep the railway going. As long as the river and later the railway were the only form of transport available, then traffic had no alternative but to move up and down the valley, but with rapid growth of road transport in the 1950s traffic tended to move at right angles to the valley. It was not a case of road taking the railway's traffic, because there are no good roads along the Severn Valley. Stourport and Bewdley tended to communicate with Kidderminster and beyond, Bridgnorth with Wolverhampton, and Ironbridge with Wellington, now part of Telford. These small towns produced little traffic, either passenger or goods, through the valley. Even had the Bridgnorth - Wolverhampton line been built, its circuitous route, like a letter 'S', would have been a disadvantage compared with the direct road. Ironbridge and Coalbrookdale together produced little passenger traffic anywhere. Yet the very drawbacks which led to closure of the railway were to become its greatest assets as a preserved branch line and tourist attraction.

From the late 1950s, when it became obvious that closure was inevitable, maintenance on the line was reduced to little more than was necessary to maintain safety, and it came as no surprise when it was announced that the line would be closed to passengers between Shrewsbury and Bewdley from 9 September 1963. The last ordinary passenger train, on Saturday 7 September, the 19.27 from Bridgnorth to Shrewsbury, was worked by Class 2 2–6–2T No 41207. A BR fishermen's special from Birmingham on Sunday 8 September, normally a diesel multiple-unit train, by special request consisted of five corridor coaches worked by 0–6–0 pannier tanks Nos 9624 and 4665. It left Bridgnorth at 18.58. Through goods traffic ended on 30 November. On the Wenlock line the Longville - Much Wenlock - Buildwas goods service finished on 2 December. On the same date the signal boxes at Hampton Loade, Bridgnorth, Coalport, Cressage and Berrington were closed. Buildwas box was closed on 15 March 1964. The track from Sutton Bridge Junction to Buildwas was retained for delivery by rail of boilers and other equipment to the new Ironbridge power station in 1965, and also for testing Rolls Royce/Sentinel diesel locomotives, as far as Berrington, until the line was closed completely on 22 January 1968.

The Woofferton - Tenbury section was closed for freight traffic on 7 October 1963 and Tenbury - Bewdley on 6 January 1964, except for the section between Bewdley and Cleobury Mortimer which remained open in connection with Admiralty traffic on the Cleobury Mortimer & Ditton Priors Light Railway. This ended on 16 April 1965 and the line was closed from 30 April. All that now remained was a passenger service between Kidderminster, Bewdley and Hartlebury; coal traffic to Stourport power station, and from Alveley colliery, and also on the line from Madeley Junction via Coalbrookdale to Buildwas power station. Coal traffic from Alveley to Buildwas ended on 30 November 1963 and southwards to Bewdley on 3 February 1969. Bewdley retained a passenger service to and from Birmingham and also to and from Hartlebury and Worcester. Withdrawal of this service was scheduled for 7 April 1969, but it was postponed because of local objections and was finally withdrawn from 5 January 1970. The last train was the 19.20 dmu from Bewdley to Kidderminster on Saturday 3 January. Bewdley North signal box was closed on 3 May 1970; Hartlebury Junction signal box on 15 May 1977. The junction was transferred to Hartlebury station signal box. Coal trains to Stourport power station travelled along a former siding beside the main line to where the Severn Valley branch turned off. This traffic ended in March 1979 and the line simply became disused. Shortly afterwards Stourport power station was shut down. On the Bewdley - Kidderminster loop BR continued to serve the sugar factory at Foley Park until 1980, but by this date, as will be seen in the next chapter, the new Severn Valley Railway had become well established.

CHAPTER 9

The New Severn Valley Railway

After closure in 1963 the section from Buildwas to Alveley Colliery sidings was abandoned. In 1964 the district engineer at Wolverhampton ordered the removal of track from Buildwas southwards for use in the enlargement of Bescot yard between Birmingham and Wolverhampton. Shortly after the job started his place was taken by Mr Roy V. Hughes who found that the line from Stourbridge Junction to Smethwick was deteriorating and was undermanned. As soon as the resident engineer at Bescot said he had enough track, Mr Hughes stopped the dismantling, which by then had reached the north end of Bridgnorth station, and he withdrew the gangers and lengthmen by trolley to Bewdley, and by train to Stourbridge Junction. Had it not been for this fortuitous action, dismantling would have continued to Alveley.

An idea for the preservation of the railway was already forming in the mind of a Kidderminster resident, Keith Beddoes, who had inspected it at Bridgnorth and Hampton Loade in April 1965 and who had made tentative enquiries. He had also considered the alternative idea of preserving the Tenbury line between Cleobury Mortimer and Bewdley, but this was unsuitable because BR could not allow access into Bewdley station at that time. A third possibility the Cleobury Mortimer & Ditton Priors Light Railway, was unsuitable because of its light axle load limits and its remoteness. Bridgnorth to Hampton Loade seemed ideal. It only needed something to stimulate the idea into action.

Notes to this chapter are on p218

On 25 June 1965 an announcement appeared in *The Kidderminster Shuttle* stating that the last through train service between Stourbridge Junction, Kidderminster and Paddington was to be withdrawn. This proved to be the stimulus that was needed. Mr Beddoes discussed his idea with a group of colleagues and friends and the outcome was a meeting of eleven people in the home of Anthony Tuite in Kidderminster on 29 June. Although there were only a few railway enthusiasts present, it was decided to hold a meeting on 6 July at the Cooper's Arms, Kidderminster[1]. About fifty attended this meeting at which it was decided to form the Severn Valley Railway Society. The secretary was Don Beddoes, brother of Keith, soon to be succeeded by A.G. Cleaver. The first chairman was Anthony Tuite and the treasurer was Columb Howell. Another, David Howley, later served on the salaried staff as deputy sales manager. Mr Tuite was replaced by J.S. Garth as acting chairman in October. A sum of £45,000 was fixed as a target for the purchase of the railway before an independent valuation was made. BR wanted a 10 per cent deposit to be paid by 4 November, by which date a contract was to be signed. It was hoped to raise the money by approaching industrial and business organisations. Fortunately the society succeeded in gaining some extra time.

There is no doubt whatever that the SVR owes its existence to Keith Beddoes. No other person came forward before he suggested the meeting and, had it been left only three weeks later, there would have been no railway to preserve and the SVR would have become another 'Dismantled Railway' marked by a broken line on the OS map. On 25 July dismantling was resumed at Bridgnorth and it was only by desperate efforts, including sending a telegram to BR headquarters, that members of the society succeeded in stopping the demolition work. That a group of amateur enthusiasts with no official status should succeed in this must have seemed incredible. Unfortunately the signal box had been demolished, but they did save the footbridge. Already they had made an inspection of the line from Bridgnorth to Hampton Loade on Sunday 11

July; a photograph of a group of eighteen pioneers appeared in *The Kidderminster Times* of Friday 16 July 1965.

The society set about with determination to purchase the disused line from Bridgnorth to Alveley Colliery Sidings, $6^1/_4$ miles, so as to operate passenger trains over the $4^1/_4$ miles between Bridgnorth and Hampton Loade. As a step towards this, the first working party was organised at Bridgnorth on 26 September 1965. On 3 February 1966 an offer of £25,000 was accepted by the BR board for land, buildings and track from Bridgnorth to a point just south of Hampton Loade, subject to contract and to the granting of a Light Railway Order by the Minister of Transport.

The next problem was raising the money. A 'Save the Severn Valley Railway Fund' was opened, into which members' subscriptions were paid. During 1966 three open week-ends were held, the first on 29-31 May when several hundreds of visitors came to Bridgnorth station and looked around the derelict site. The only steam activity was a steam roller in the yard. On 9-10 July nearly 1,000 came, at an entrance fee of 1s. 6d each. The following occasion, 24-25 September, a fairground was set up and 1,500 visitors came. At all these events sales stands raised considerable sums.

In the Newsletter of October 1966 the secretary, A.G. Cleaver, was able to state that £1,150 had been paid to BR to obtain possession of the whole Bridgnorth station site. The first Annual General Meeting of the SVR Society was held at Bridgnorth station on 26 November 1966. Various officers were appointed or re-appointed, and Richard Dunn became the society's solicitor.

On 8 February 1967 the society paid £2,500 to BR as a 10 per cent deposit on the purchase price, but to complete the purchase a limited company had to be formed. For this purpose the Severn Valley Railway Co Ltd was incorporated on 24 May under the Companies Act 1948. It was limited by guarantee only and had no share capital, so it would not be possible for any one member or third party to buy voting control of the company by acquiring a majority of shares. The

'Memorandum and Articles of Association' dated 1 May 1967 set out the objects of the company which were: 'to preserve, retain and restore the standard-gauge railway extending from Bridgnorth to Kidderminster via Bewdley in the counties of Salop and Worcester or any parts thereof and for such purpose to purchase, take upon lease, or otherwise acquire from the British Railways Board the said railway or part or parts thereof and the lands, works, buildings, track, stock, machinery and rights relating thereto.'

It will be noted that even at this early stage the company aimed to preserve and restore the line right through to Kidderminster. Other objects were: to acquire rights and privileges, to dispose of unwanted assets, to produce timetables, books, etc, to operate and maintain steam locomotives, rolling stock and other equipment necessary to operate a train service, to carry passengers and goods, to provide workshops and refreshment facilities; to apply to the Ministry of Transport for an order to enable the company to carry out these objects, and to make by-laws and regulations. The liability of the members was limited and in the event of the company being wound up the members could not be called upon for payment of over one pound. The seven subscribers to the company were: K.S. Beddoes, A.G. Bending, J.A. Bodfish, A.G. Cleaver, J.R. Colbourn, R.H. Dunn and D.C. Williams.

The last became editor of the house magazine, *Severn Valley Railway News* which he has edited quarterly from issue 3 in July 1966. The first two issues, edited by Paul C. Wyers, appeared in November 1965 and March 1966. Issues 1 - 10 were duplicated on quarto sheets, but from issue No 11, January 1969, the journal was printed by W.J. Ray & Co of Walsall.

Contracts were exchanged with BR on 1 January 1967, on the condition that the Light Railway Order was obtained. In September 1967 it was announced that Edwards, Blackie & Co of Newhall Street, Birmingham, had been appointed consulting civil engineers for the society. Open days in 1967 drew even greater numbers. On 25 March the arrival of 0–6–0 3205 with four coaches marked the start of a three-day event which drew several thousand visitors. The engine and two coaches made trips to Oldbury viaduct and back. At another weekend on 6-7 May 2-6-0 46443 was in steam, and on 24 - 25 June 1967, even though no engines were moved, visitors added £225 to the funds. The first of the 'normal' weekends was on 14 - 15 October when the two engines worked a four-coach train continually. Vast numbers of people attended, as shown in the photograph on page 80. Since only members of the Society could travel on the railway, passengers were enabled to travel by obtaining 'day membership' tickets by which they became members of the Society on the day of the journey only.

The Light Railways Acts of 1896 and 1912 made provision for a railway to be built or, by way of reducing costs, for an existing railway to be worked, as a 'Light Railway', so making it unnecessary to obtain an individual Act of Parliament at a cost of many thousands of pounds. For the SVR to become a 'Light Railway' it was necessary for the owners of the line, BR, to obtain the LRO and later to obtain a Transfer Order transferring the powers of the LRO to the SVR Co Ltd when the latter had purchased the line.

The application for the LRO was completed at the end of 1967. Its publication by BR on 1 February 1968 brought forth objections from Highley Rural District Council who complained of a narrow bridge at Eardington, and from Shropshire County Council because of the expense of building a railway bridge over the proposed Bridgnorth by-pass at an estimated cost of £50,000 to £60,000. The impending closure of Highley colliery was announced on 15 November 1967, and it was clear that Alveley colliery would close in the near future. The extension of the SVR scheme to Bewdley became a distinct possibility.

On 2 December 1967 the Society held its second AGM. Membership of both the Society and the Company had continued to grow and by the end of 1967 the Society had around 900 members and the Company 200.

An important influence in the development of professionalism and discipline was provided by two local BR officers:

Gordon Keeling and William Gillett, both ex GWR men. The late Mr Keeling was concerned with signalling and movement of rolling stock onto the SVR. Mr Gillett, who began his career on the GWR in 1927, and who was concerned with operational safety and signalling in the Birmingham Division of BR, was instrumental in facilitating storage of SVR stock and the carrying out of restoration work at Bewdley while BR was still in possession of the site. Another BR man, Philip Coutanche, gave much assistance in the early days of the railway. They are mentioned as a token of the gratitude of the older SVR members for their help.

During 1968 there was progress both on the railway and behind the scenes. On Sunday 31 March a party of senior BR officers including Mr R.C. Bray, chief surveyor of BR, and Mr T.D. Cook, LM Region surveyor, made a trip from Bridgnorth to Bewdley and back behind 0–6–0 3205. Afterwards Mr Bray commented: 'The Company have more than demonstrated their competence to run a railway, and they are not playing trains. I like the job they have done.'

At another steam weekend on 13 - 14 April hundreds of 'day members' made the journey from Bridgnorth to Hampton Loade and back behind 3205 and 46443. More money was raised by a great number of sales stands. During the three days 31 August - 2 September two five-coach trains ran between Bridgnorth and Hampton Loade. Over 10,000 visitors attended.

Because of the objections to the application for the LRO the Minister of Transport, Richard Marsh, ordered a public inquiry which was held at the Shire Hall, Abbey Foregate, Shrewsbury, on 1 - 2 October 1968. Over 100 members and supporters attended and many gave evidence of which there was 122 foolscap pages.[2] The result of the inquiry, reached on 6 June 1969, was that the application should be granted, and the Council's objections were dismissed. However, the Minister took the extraordinary step of overruling his inspector's decision and refused the application because of the Council's objection, but he left the way open for the company to negotiate with the County Council. Meanwhile consent to occupy the line between Alveley and Bewdley North box had been obtained in May 1969.

On 6 November 1968 Highley colliery closed completely. Winding of coal but not of men had ended here soon after Alveley colliery was opened in 1937, but this too was closed on 31 January 1969. Coal traffic finished at the end of March and the line from Alveley to Bewdley became disused. It had been expected that Alveley colliery, a modern establishment, would remain in production much longer, so giving the SVR the opportunity to consolidate its position. Coming so soon, even before the LRO had been obtained, the company was placed in a difficult situation because if the southern section was to be secured, and with it the connection to the main BR network, no time could be lost. Because of the senseless ban on the operation of steam locomotives, then in force on BR, and because the line was still BR property, it was not possible to operate trains in 1969 and an important source of revenue was lost. But other activities continued.

BR undertook a valuation survey on the Bewdley - Alveley section and completed this in August 1969. Support for the railway continued to increase and on 10 June membership of the Society was 1,569. A further step at this time was occupation by the SVR of Bridgnorth goods shed, on payment of a further £2,000 to BR. Salop County Council kept up its delaying tactics concerning the bridge over the Brignorth by-pass. On 16 September 1969 the county surveyor, Mr Mare, stated that visibility at the bridge over the Cleobury Mortimer road, just south of Bridgnorth station, was substandard and he required removal of an abutment. In the end it had to be agreed that nothing could be done to improve the situation here. It was decided that the SVR Co should provide the bridge over the by-pass at its own expense and in November it was announced that the County Council had withdrawn its main objection to the LRO. On 4 December the new Minister of Transport, Frederick Mulley, stated that the order would be granted.

On 10 November 1969 Viscount Garnock was appointed 'prestige director' in the Guarantee Company to give it the benefit of his wide business experience and influence. An important step was taken on 6 December when it was decided to merge the SVR Society and the Company. The amalgamation was confirmed on 31 December. The British Railways Board (Severn Valley) Light Railway Order 1970 was made on 5 January, (the same date as the withdrawal of passenger trains to Bewdley) to come into operation on 16 January. It authorised the BRB to work as a light railway the line from 8 yards north of milepost $144^1/_2$ ($^3/_4$ mile north of Alveley Colliery Halt) to the western boundary of Hollybush Road in Bridgnorth. Two days later the company filed its application for the Transfer Order.

One result of the success in obtaining the LRO seems to have been a large increase in membership, from 1,650 on 1 February to 1,899 on 21 April 1970. In August 1971 Mr Leslie Harvey took upon himself the work of membership secretary, at a time when membership had reached about 3,000. He continued in the work until 1984 when the membership, by then over 13,000, was transferred to a computer. He retired, aged nearly 80, having for many years given over thirty hours a week to the work, even finding time to write personal letters to some members. Few volunteers could have done more.

On 14 March the railway was visited by Major P.M. Olver, one of the inspecting officers of railways for the Ministry of Transport. He was greatly impressed by the standards achieved by the company. The Severn Valley Light Railway (Transfer) Order 1970 was made on 20 May. On Saturday 23rd regular passenger services began; the first train, six GWR coaches behind 0–6–0 3205, left Bridgnorth at 14.00. An hourly service was operated between Bridgnorth and Hampton Loade. However, because of delay in printing the Transfer Order at H M Stationery Office, the service had to be suspended on the weekends of 13-14 and 20-21 June 1970, although by then 3,000 passengers had been safely carried.

Another technical problem now arose. Although the SVR

Co Ltd had received authority from the Railways Inspectorate of the Ministry of Transport to run trains as soon as the Light Railway Order was signed, the company later received a letter from the legal department of the Ministry pointing out that, under Clause 3 (2) of the Transfer Order, the Order became effective only on the transfer of all the assets of the railway to the Company on completion of payment of the £25,000. At the date of the Order £4,500 had been paid to BR. The balance of £20,500 was found by the SVR board from:

1	'Save the SVR Fund'	£12,000
2	Trading Income	1,200
3	Bank overdraft secured by the board's guarantee	3,000
4	Loans from two members	4,300
		£20,500

The sum was paid to BR on 24 June 1970 and the line from Bridgnorth to Hampton Loade became the property of the SVR Co Ltd. This left a sum of £7,300 to be repaid as soon as possible. Weekend services were resumed from 27 June.

On 25 October 1970 Viscount Cobham of Hagley Hall visited the SVR and agreed to become president. In the meantime progress had been made towards the purchase of the southern section of the line and, apart from some legal and financial details, negotiations were concluded between the BR board and the SVR Co Ltd for the latter to purchase the line from Hampton Loade to Kidderminster Junction. At a meeting between representatives of the SVR Co Ltd and BR Estates Department on 15 October 1970 the price of £74,000 was accepted for the section from milepost 144½ at Alveley to 200 yards east of Foley Park Halt, a length of 8½ miles. This sum was made up of £25,000 for land and £49,000 for track, stations, equipment, etc. An agreement with BR to pay this amount was signed on 16 February 1971.

At this stage the company enlisted the support of Sir Gerald Nabarro, MP for Worcestershire South since 1961 and before that for Kidderminster, a man of wide experience in business and politics whose advice, coupled with his enthusiasm for railways, was seen as a great asset to the railway. In 1961 he had opposed the closure of the Bewdley - Tenbury - Woofferton line for which, however, there was no hope, and then had urged the use of its route for a Bewdley by-pass. He also opposed closure of the SVR. He was appointed an additional director of the Guarantee Company on 1 November 1970. At about the same time he wrote a book, *Severn Valley Steam*, using material supplied by David Williams, editor of the *Severn Valley Railway News*, and by others. This was launched with some pomp at the Great Western Royal Hotel at Paddington on 6 July 1971 when Nabarro was introduced by Mr J. Bonham-Carter, general manager of the Western Region of BR.

The third AGM of the Company was held at Bridgnorth on 1 May 1971. Sir Gerald Nabarro outlined his proposals for reopening the railway to Bewdley and Foley Park, for which £150,000 was to be raised. He dismissed the idea of a trust corporation and proposed to form a public company, the Severn Valley Railway (Holdings) Co. It was expected that £75,000 would be required in twelve to eighteen months to purchase the railway. In addition £50,000 would be needed for the by-pass bridge and £25,000 for operating capital. Already Nabarro could be seen taking over control of the railway. The meeting was adjourned until 6 August. On 2 July the chairman, A.B. Marsden Smedley, sent out a personal letter to all the members explaining the situtión. He considered it would be necessary to wind up the Guarantee Company and to re-form it as a company limited by share capital. In exchange for its assets the members of the Guarantee Company would be allocated 40,000 shares free of charge. The balance of 110,000 shares would be offered at par for cash at £1 each by private subscription. To facilitate formation of the new company, Mr Marsden Smedley agreed to retire as chairman to be replaced by Sir Gerald Nabarro.

Members were now becoming alarmed at the developments

and there were mutterings about a dictatorship. A meeting of former committee members of the SVR Society was held on 2 July to discuss the formation of a Severn Valley Railway Association to protect the interests of members. At a meeting of the members at Bridgnorth on 17 July this proposal was put forward and was accepted and a provisional committee was elected. At its first meeting in Bridgnorth on Saturday 16 October Mr J.S. Garth was elected chairman. He explained that formation of the Association resulted from a concern for the future of the SVR following proposals to operate it on a purely commercial basis.

What was being overlooked was that there are grave dangers in seeking to make a commercial organisation out of a body which depends for its success on the co-operation of a large number of subscribing volunteers. These form an exceedingly powerful force over which management has no control. By virtue of the fact that the workers are unpaid - indeed paying - members, they can refuse with impunity to co-operate if something displeases them. They can simply turn their backs on the railway and go somewhere else, or apply their skills in non-operational work, having lost nothing.

That the volunteers do not abuse their power is largely because their work on the railway is their hobby: they are amateur railwaymen in the literal sense that they do the work for the love of it. Among them are many professional engineers, drivers, guards, signalmen and other railwaymen who work on the SVR in their spare time. The debt which the railway owes to these enthusiasts cannot be stated in financial terms. Of course, only a small portion of the total membership can, or will, be active volunteers. As a whole the membership makes a substantial financial contribution: for example, in 1986, members' subscriptions brought in a clear profit of over £23,000 after deducting the *SVR News* (included in the subscription) and administrative expenses. Many members, not railway enthusiasts, join simply to give their support. They may be active in another railway society or live at such a distance that the expense and time involved in visiting the railway is too much. Others maintain their support despite advancing years or other problems. Non-active subscribers cannot be dismissed as 'armchair members'. The SVR is fortunate in always having had a substantial body of dedicated volunteers prepared to give their diverse skills, and their time and energy, to the successful working of the railway; but there are never enough, and the management cannot afford to abuse them.

The adjourned AGM was held at Bridgnorth on 6 August 1971 and was attended by over 300 members. The meeting approved the alteration of the SVR structure to enable money to be raised by share issue and Sir Gerald Nabarro spoke at length on the subject. He considered that the immediate aim should be to raise about £110,000 of which £74,000 was for purchase of the railway and £36,000 for working capital.

At the board meeting on 7 September 1971 Nabarro was appointed chairman of the company and A.B. Marsden Smedley retired as a director after having steered the railway through many difficult situations.

In the summer of 1971 the experiment was tried for the first time in running a daily train service between Bridgnorth and Hampton Loade from 26 July to 8 August, with considerable success. On 8 August the 100,000th passenger for the year was carried. For 1970 the total number had been 63,000. At a ceremony at Bridgnorth station on 12 September Class 5 4–6–0 45110 was officially named *RAF Biggin Hill.* As a publicity stunt it may have succeeded, but the name was never popular among the volunteers; notices even appeared stating that the practice of removing the nameplates must cease. From 7 March to 31 December 1971 over 171,000 passenger journeys were made, at a fare of 45p return first class or 30p return second (or third as it is still known on the SVR).

On 5 November 1971 the BR board signed a provisional contract agreeing to sell to the SVR Co all the land occupied by the southern section of the line for £25,000; and a separate contract, dated 29 January 1972, covered the track, buildings and engineering works for a price of £49,000, making the agreed total of £74,000. Deposits of £5,000 were paid by the SVR Co on both contracts.

The Severn Valley Railway (Holdings) Company was incorporated as a private company on 15 March 1972 with Sir Gerald Nabarro as chairman. The prospectus inviting subscriptions for capital bore the caption: 'Buy shares of £1 each in Severn Valley Railway (Holdings) Ltd and contribute to the restoration of a public steam railway service for tourists, passengers and freight between Kidderminster, Bewdley and Bridgnorth on the Severn Valley Line.' Tourists, apparently, were not passengers. The authorised capital was £150,000 in 150,000 shares of £1 each, of which 100,000 were to be issued, followed by a rights issue of 50,000. Of the 100,000 shares, 2,000 had been issued already, 58,000 were offered to the public and 40,000 were allotted to the Guarantee Company, which continued its existence, in exchange for its assets. The fixed assets of the SVR Co at 31 December 1971 were:

	£
Freehold land, buildings and permanent way	26,502
Locomotives, rolling stock and equipment	17,975
Office furniture and equipment	364
	44,841

The reserves totalled £42,910 and included the Save the SVR Fund, £19,326, and the Bridgnorth By-pass Bridge Fund, £2,995. Two directors of the Guarantee Company were appointed to the board of the Holdings Company as trustees of their company's interests. The minimum subscription was £5 and the maximum £5,000. For three weeks, from 12 April until 3 May 1972, shares were issued to members only; afterwards they were offered to the public, and the share offer was closed on 22 May.

The prospectus disclosed the interests of directors and mentioned that 'On 29 March 1971 a contract was concluded between the Guarantee Company and Sir Gerald David Nunes Nabarro MP and Sir Gerald Nabarro (Publications) Ltd for resale over a period of five years expiring on 29 March 1976, a total of 3,750 copies of *Severn Valley Steam* at a total wholesale price of £3,625, of which about 20 per cent have been taken to date.' In the end the stock had to be remaindered at 75p a copy.

The share offer was over-subscribed by a total of £24,690 which was returned to the non-preferential subscribers. This caused considerable ill-feeling among a large number of people who had wished to support the project but who had found their offer rejected. It was thought by many that much goodwill towards the railway was thereby lost and that a better way could have been found to deal with these subscriptions. The level of support had been underestimated.

On 16 March 1972, the day after the incorporation of the Holdings Co, an agreement was concluded between the Holdings and Guarantee companies, on the condition that the minimum subscription was raised. Following this the assets and liabilities of the Guarantee Co, including the northern section of the line and the benefit of the contracts to purchase the southern section, would be transferred to the Holdings Co in exchange for the 40,000 shares credited as fully paid up. The Holdings Co, as owner of the railway, would retain all revenue from operations and would be responsible for all maintenance costs and payment of staff. It would exercise control over financial matters and purchase of rolling stock, locomotives, track and other assets. The Guarantee Co would remain responsible for operating the railway. All workers on the railway must be members of the Guarantee Co in order to be covered by insurance. The 'rights' issue, made in July 1972, offered shareholders one further share for cash at par for every two held, to raise a further £50,000 to finance completion of purchase of the land and the railway. By 30 December the full amount was subscribed. The next task was to obtain a Light Railway Order.

At the fourth AGM of the Guarantee Co at Bridgnorth on 3 November 1972 it was clear that all was not well with the relationship between the volunteers and the Holdings Co.

Nabarro wanted to have the line opened to Bewdley in 1973 but the Light Railway Order would not be granted until the signalling was completed on the northern section, the Victoria Bridge reconstructed, the loop installed at Arley, protection provided at Northwood Crossing, and various works carried out at Bewdley. The civil engineer said that his department had insufficient time to install watering facilities at Bewdley. The departmental manager's advice that the opening should be postponed for a year had been ignored. Mr Garth, chairman of the SVR Association, thought it unfair that the assets of the Guarantee Co should be exchanged for pieces of paper for which the voting rights would be held by the Holdings Board. There was great dissatisfaction with the agreement of 16 March between the two companies, in particular the appointment by the Holdings Co of six directors and the chairman of the Guarantee Co out of a proposed total of twelve directors. These provisions were rejected by the Association. In view of members' concern about the future of Bridgnorth station, no final decision was to be made about the by-pass bridge without the approval of a properly convened extraordinary general meeting. Applications for positions on the railway's paid staff should be invited from the members. There were calls for the resignation of the chairman, but Nabarro refused to resign until his task was completed, at the next AGM.

A note from Nabarro in *SVR News* No 26, Winter 1972-3, stated that the subscription of £150,000 capital was completed on 30 December 1972, including the rights issue of £50,000. The southern section had been purchased from BR, subject to the granting of the LRO.

A new contract was drawn up between the two companies and the SVR Association and was signed on 24 February 1973; at the same time the constitution of the SVR Association was approved by the Guarantee Co Board which could now nominate two directors to the Holdings Co board and the Association could nominate one. The maximum number of directors of the Holdings Co was to be increased accordingly. The following directors were appointed to the board of the

Holdings Co from 1 January 1973: M.J. Draper, T.J. Holder and T.J. Willis.

A period of turmoil now overtook the railway, involving disputes between Sir Gerald Nabarro and the volunteer workers. On 2 January 1973 one of the above directors, Mr. T.J. Willis, a property developer, appeared on the share register as having 15,000 shares. On 30 May he bought 200 more so that he now held $12^1/_2$ per cent of the SVR shares. At the same time, realising the tremendous property value of the Bridgnorth station site, and in view of the possibility of the railway being unable to finance the bridge over the by-pass, Nabarro had the station site valued, ostensibly so as to know how much to expect from its sale should the company be forced to abandon it. The members, probably correctly, saw this as a threat to sell off the site, particularly in view of the construction of the run-round loop at Eardington, installed by contractors at a cost of £8,000, (with a connection at the north end too tight for most locomotives, which was later removed). Detailed plans were in fact prepared for the enlargement of Eardington station and provision of a car park, but little was revealed about this. Also it appeared unlikely that Willis as a property developer would have invested so heavily in the railway without prospect of gain. Another matter leading to suspicion was the removal of the headquarters of the railway from Bridgnorth to Bewdley, notwithstanding that the Bewdley building, incorporating the stationmaster's house, had more rooms. The company's stance in the matter as revealed later in Mr Dunn's article in *SVR News* No 27, Spring 1973, made it clear that it was fully prepared to sell the Bridgnorth station site.

Another matter which annoyed the volunteers was the painting of Bewdley station, at a cost of £1,500, which the volunteers had offered to do for the cost of materials. Also Nabarro had used £6,000 of the company's assets to obtain GWR 4–6–0 4930 *Hagley Hall* in June 1972. The engine arrived at Bewdley from Woodham's scrapyard at Barry on 6 January 1973. At the time it was too heavy to be used on the railway, though with a total weight of 75 tons and an axle load of 18 tons 19cwt, it may be asked why it was considered too heavy when *Britannia*, already at Bridgnorth, weighed 94 tons with an axle load of 20 tons 5cwt, but this was not owned by the SVR and was not allowed over Victoria Bridge with a full boiler. The result was a dispute between Nabarro and Mr Dunn who had proposed private purchase of *Hagley Hall*. There were difficulties, too, with the operating superintendent Arthur Stewart-Becker, a salaried member of the railway staff, with whom some volunteers had not been working amicably. Nevertheless, his dismissal caused an uproar among the volunteers who threatened to refuse to operate the railway unless Nabarro resigned. On one occasion Nabarro was heard to exclaim 'I'm not going to be pushed around by a pack of volunteers!' Another time he greeted Keith Beddoes saying 'Hello Mr Beddoes! Look at what I've done with your railway!' This was hardly the attitude to win the support of the volunteers who had given so much of their time and energy to the reconstruction and operation of the railway.

The board of the Guarantee Co held a special meeting on 11 March 1973 to consider the dispute between Sir Gerald Nabarro and the volunteers. At a long joint meeting of the boards of the two companies on 17 March Sir Gerald defended his position, saying that the company had only £10,000 of overdraft facilities and £50,000 of debt. At the same time he claimed that under his chairmanship the company made a trading profit of £7,500 in its first ten months to 31 December 1972, solely due to his management.[3] After the meeting the following notice appeared. It was printed in the *SVR News* No 27, Spring 1973.

RAILWAY SAFETY

'The Becker Incident' received great publicity in the newspapers recently. Here are some further relevant facts.

Mr Becker has stated that he wrote to the Parliamentary Inspectorate in the interests of railway safety after the Board had resolved at Sir Gerald Nabarro's instigation that Mr Becker as operating Superintendent should have no contact with the Railway Inspectorate as he had done over the past year. This order of events would preclude him from successfully contesting his dismissal in a Court, which would only be concerned with chronological facts and would ignore the important and related political and other factors. Only in this context does Mr Becker accept the situation, and still considers that the action was unfair and out of proportion to the supposed crime and that the matter would have been amicably resolved otherwise had the political and other factors of such major importance to the former Chairman not been predominant, and had he in accordance with the principles of natural justice been given the opportunity of speaking in his defence to the Holdings Board.

Bearing the above facts in mind, here is the official press statement issued after the crucial combined Boards' meeting at Bewdley on 17 March:-

SEVERN VALLEY RAILWAY (HOLDINGS) LTD.
AND SEVERN VALLEY RAILWAY CO. LTD.

An agreed statement, signed by Sir Gerald Nabarro, MP, at 4.0 p.m., on Saturday, 17 March 1973 for issue to the Press and all others concerned.

1. Mr A.F.S. Becker accepts his dismissal and confirms his offer to continue as Shedmaster of the line as a volunteer and become Acting Operating Superintendent of the line until the date of the First Annual General Meeting of the Holdings Company, or until the appointment of a properly qualified full-time replacement acceptable to both Boards.
2. Sir Gerald Nabarro steps down as Chairman of the Boards of Directors of Severn Valley Railway (Holdings) Limited and Severn Valley Railway Company Limited, until the date of the First Annual General Meeting of the Holdings Company, at which time he will offer himself for re-election to the Board of the Holdings Company, and in the meantime will remain a Director of both Companies.

3. The Directors of both Companies have agreed to accept these offers.
4. It is hoped that work will continue on the line with a view to the commencement of the scheduled services.
5. The Directors of the Holdings Company have elected the Viscount Garnock to be Chairman, and Mr R.H. Dunn continues as Deputy Chairman.
6. The Directors of the Guarantee Company have elected Mr R.H. Dunn to be Chairman, and Lt Cdr H.C.C. Mossop as Deputy Chairman.

In addition, other important decisions were taken:

a. The two properly proposed nominees of the Guarantee Board, Mr D.E. Guest and Mr C.R.P. Ridgway receive the approval of the Holdings Board, and become members of the Holdings Board.
b. Provision is now made for a representative of the Severn Valley Railway Association to 'sit in' at Holdings Board meetings.

So Mr Dunn took over the chairmanship of the Guarantee Co and Messrs Guest and Ridgway joined the Holdings Board as nominees of the Guarantee Co to be trustees of the Guarantee Co's shares. On 24 May Sir Gerald Nabarro resigned from the boards of both companies. He was then a sick man, having suffered a heart attack. On 29 June 1973 *The Times* published a long article about his resignation and his career with the SVR. That day was also his 60th birthday, his last. On 18 November he died at his home at Broadway, Worcestershire, where he had lived since 1950.

At this distance in time it can be seen that there was a lack of direct communication and explanation with an extremely diversified work force. But there can be little doubt now that Nabarro's role was invaluable in securing the future of the railway at a difficult period when a large sum of money was needed quickly. His downfall resulted from finding himself in a position of power and authority, which he used with insufficient regard for the strength of the volunteers.

While all this was happening progress was being made towards obtaining the LRO. Again this had to be made in the name of British Railways and later transferred to the SVR. The British Railways Board (Severn Valley) Light Railway Order 1973 was made on 27 February and it came into operation on the 28th. It authorised BR to work as light railways, first, the section from the southern end of the previously authorised light railway at Alveley to a point 247 yards east of the Bridge carrying the A451 Kidderminster - Stourport road over the Bewdley - Kidderminster loop line, and, second, the section of the original SVR from Bewdley to a point 302 yards south of the southern portal of Mount Pleasant tunnel, notwithstanding that this section, which had been bought for an additional £100, was dismantled.

Another development close by, with which the SVR originally considered co-operating, was the opening of the Wild Life Park, later known as the West Midlands Safari Park, on 16 April 1973. There was even a suggestion of a station to serve it, but since its visitors have to be inside vehicles and come in cars and coaches, it is doubtful if the station would have benefited either the park or the railway.

Throughout all this period the unresolved question of the Bridgnorth by-pass bridge hung threateningly over the affairs of the railway. Little was it realised that yet another decade was to pass before it was built. An Extraordinary General Meeting of the Guarantee Co was held at Bridgnorth on 18 May 1973 to discuss the bridge. The facts of the case were put before the members in an article to *SVR News* No 27, Spring 1973, by R.H. Dunn, in which he presented a strong argument in favour of abandoning the Bridgnorth station site. Looking back on it about 15 years later it seems extraordinary that this could ever have been considered, but Mr Dunn stated that its sale could raise £150,000 and with the cost of the bridge, £70,000, this would be the equivalent of spending £220,000 which would be enough to finance the rest of the railway. The argument, as can now be seen, had two flaws. First, one could hardly count the £150,000 on the station site as expenditure when it consisted of nothing more than a valuation and, second, the loss to the railway of a northern terminus in an attractive town of considerable size would have far outweighed any monetary gain which might have accrued from its sale. Neither Hampton Loade nor Eardington could be considered as termini because of access and parking difficulties, and there was no suitable space between Oldbury viaduct and the route of the by-pass where a new station could be established nearer to Bridgnorth. The true fact, not mentioned at the meeting, was that even with the cost of the bridge added to what had been paid for the Bridgnorth station site, the SVR had obtained a bargain. Fortunately sound sense won the day and at the end of the meeting the vote to retain Bridgnorth station and to raise money for the bridge was almost unanimous. Since then Bridgnorth station site has generated millions of pounds. It is an interesting thought that the estimated cost of the bridge almost equalled the sum paid for the entire railway from Alveley to Foley Park, including Victoria Bridge, three viaducts and Bewdley tunnel. But it is clear now that BR was unloading onto the SVR, not simply track, buildings and works, but the maintenance problems and expense connected with them. These have indeed proved a considerable burden and could, without careful and far-seeing direction, bring about the downfall of the railway.

Following withdrawal of BR passenger services to Bewdley in January 1970, many types of BR diesel locomotives came through to Bewdley via Kidderminster bringing old rolling stock and locomotives. This proved a great help in establishing the good relations with BR which have always been a feature of SVR operation. At Christmas 1972 a new experiment was tried in running trains on Saturday and Sunday 22 and 23 December, but Father Christmas had not yet arrived. Trains also ran from Boxing Day until 30 December. During 1973 the SVR made an operating loss of £24,000, mainly on outgoings on the 12¾ miles from Bridgnorth to Bewdley, when earnings were coming from operations on only the 4½ miles from Bridgnorth to Hampton Loade. It remained to be seen if the return fare of £1 decided upon for Bridgnorth to Bewdley, and certainly high for the period, would deter passengers from making the journey.

Great progress was made in the operation of the railway in 1973. The signal box and signalling at Hampton Loade was commissioned during May and on 2 June electric train token working began between there and Bridgnorth. Later in the year a telephone link was established between Hampton Loade and Highley after cable laying and installation of new signalling equipment at Highley. Early in 1974 Highley signal-box was re-commissioned and electric train token working was established between there and Hampton Loade.

An important event in SVR history was the signing, in December 1973, of an agreement with Rubery Owen Holdings Ltd who were to take out 150,000 shares in the SVR (Holdings) Co. A first loan instalment of £50,000 was received in December with a promise of further instalments of £10,000 as required up to 31 March 1974. The original idea was that the SVR would restore the Hollybush Road footbridge at Bridgnorth which was built by the predecessors of Rubery Owen but, as explained in chapter 6, this was too expensive. The Guarantee Co also applied for a further £5,000 shares; £4,000 was already on loan to the Holdings Co and the remaining £1,000 came from cash at the bank. On 29 March the share capital of the company was increased to £550,000.

Authority to work the railway to Bewdley and beyond came with the Severn Valley Light Railway (Transfer) Order 1974, made on 28 March and coming into operation on the 29th. It ruled that weights and speeds might be limited by the Minister of Transport and it forbade the carrying of passengers until permission of the Minister had been obtained. Any contravention of these provisions rendered the company liable to a penalty 'not exceeding twenty pounds'.

The first passenger train to Highley left Bridgnorth on Good Friday, 12 April 1974, behind WD 2–10–0 No 600 *Gordon*. Three trains ran at 45 minute intervals, crossing at Hampton Loade, with 20min for reversal at Highley. Before trains could run farther, an iron bridge over the lane just beyond Highley had to be rebuilt. The iron beams of this 32ft span bridge, cast at Brymbo in 1861, had corroded, but delivery of the replacement steelwork had been delayed by the effect of the three-day working week then in force, and a fuel shortage. Also, Edwards & Blackie, the SVR consulting civil engineers, were preparing a report for submission to the Department of the Environment on the condition of the Victoria Bridge.

Major Olver inspected the line to Bewdley on 16 May and recommended the DoE to sanction opening. On Saturday 18 May passenger trains began running through to Bewdley. The inaugural passenger trip from Bridgnorth was made by GWR railcar No 22. The first steam train left Bewdley behind 0–6–0PT 5764. From Bridgnorth the first steam train was hauled by 2–6–0 43106. A shuttle service was retained between Bridgnorth and Hampton Loade, for which the return fare was 40p. A more intensive service south of here had to await completion of the loop at Arley.

At the beginning of June 1974 membership of the Guarantee Co reached 5,000. The half-fare concession to members may have had some influence on the increase in membership; with higher fares for the longer journey a member could quickly recover the cost of his membership. The number of members continued to grow: it reached 6,000 early in 1977, 8,050 on 1 November 1978, 8,548 on 31 May 1979, and 9,029 on 31 December 1979.

Changes in the Holdings Board occurred over the years. At the AGM on 9 May 1975 John Garth succeeded Richard Dunn as deputy chairman and in 1976 Lord Garnock resigned the chair for business reasons but remained a director, and he was succeeded by W.B. (Bill) Broadbent. On 31 January 1976 Lt Cdr H.C.C. Mossop resigned as general manager and Michael Draper became acting general manager, and general manager later that year. At the AGM in 1977 Lord Garnock (now the Earl of Lindsay) retired from the Holdings Board and accepted the title of President in succession to Lord Cobham who died that year. At the AGM of the Guarantee Co on 21

July 1979 John Garth resigned from the board but remained on the board of the Holdings Co. He was succeeded as chairman by D.C. Williams, editor of the *SVR News*.

With management always on the lookout for new ways of generating income, no opportunity was lost to offer the use of the railway for films and television. One, which was not much success as a film, was *The Seven per cent Solution* based on a Sherlock Holmes story, but not by Conan Doyle. For this purpose track was relaid during September 1975 on the abandoned Stourport section from Bewdley to within 300 yards of Mount Pleasant tunnel, to allow shots of trains approaching on two converging lines. The track was afterwards removed.

A great annual attraction became established in December 1975 when Father Christmas installed 'himself' (actually more than one) at Arley and a shuttle service was operated between there and Bewdley. The fare included a present for the children, or hot punch for the adults. The idea for this came from the Keighley & Worth Valley Railway, as also did the highly successful 'Enthusiasts' Weekends'.

Arley loop was completed in 1976 and was passed by Major Olver. On 25 March 1977 he inspected the extension to Foley Park and authorised the running of passenger trains which had to have a locomotive at each end because of lack of run-round facilities. Trains were run to Foley Park on gala days only, such as enthusiasts' weekends. Following the course of inflation the Bridgnorth - Bewdley return fare became £1.80. With a view to running heavier locomotives the track was constantly being upgraded. At the end of 1976 the upgrading scheme was approved by the Manpower Services Commission and extra labour became available on the track early in 1977. By the following year the track was sufficiently improved to enable 4–6–0 6960 *Raveningham Hall* to run over the line, subject to a few restrictions.

Of outstanding importance at this period were the several trains run from Bridgnorth to places on BR, using SVR-based Great Western coaches. From 1976 trains were run to Paddington, Chester (using 6000 *King George V* and 6201 *Princess*

Elizabeth between there and Hereford), Plymouth, Kingswear and Pwllheli. Two important developments in 1979 are worth mentioning: on 5 May the Monmouthshire Railway Society operated a special from Cardiff onto the SVR, the first through train from BR; and on four Saturdays in August, as an experiment, BR operated a dmu service between Kidderminster and Bewdley. The popularity of this justified its continuation in the four following years. At the celebration at Shildon in August 1975 to commemorate the 150th anniversary of the Stockton & Darlington Railway, and at Rainhill in May 1980 for the 150th anniversary of the Liverpool & Manchester Railway, the SVR was well represented, by locomotives and coaches, and yet still had enough motive power to operate its services, though with little to spare. Membership of the Guarantee Co continued to grow; at the AGM on 28 June 1980 members were told that it had reached 10,006, five figures at last! By the end of the year it was 10,335.

That threatening old bogey, the Bridgnorth by-pass bridge scheme, emerged again in 1980. At the 12th AGM of the Guarantee Co on 28 June 1980 it was noted that Shropshire County Council was at last pushing forward plans for the by-pass. But encouragement was to be had from recent costings which had shown that reduction in the original planned width of the road would halve the cost of the bridge, and that it could be covered by the existing bank facilities of the Holdings Co. The Guarantee Co had £2,995 in its By-pass Bridge Fund. The protracted delay had served a purpose in that it had enabled the SVR to become firmly established in the district, with a good deal of strength and with the same kind of prestige as the Ironbridge Gorge Museum. No doubt the county authorities realised that it was now a power to be reckoned with and that the customary bullying tactics would not get them far. Meanwhile plans were prepared for the bridge and a programme was worked out.

By negotiations through the County Council and central Government, and in view of the progress of inflation since the SVR was established, a contract was made between the SVR

(Holdings) Co and Shropshire County Council on 25 January 1982 whereby the SVR would pay only 30 per cent of the cost of the bridge, and would act as agent for the construction. Its consulting engineers Edwards & Blackie were given responsibility for the design; Rubery Owen Steelwork Ltd were to fabricate the steelwork, and the construction contract was given to E.E. Jeavons, a local firm of contractors. Contracts were signed in 1982; on 31 October the track was removed by SVR volunteers and on 1 November work began on clearing the embankment. After the wettest October for twenty years it was muddy work removing about 2000m^3 of earth. Abutments and wing walls consumed 300m^3 (750 tons) of concrete and were ready by Christmas. The girders, each weighing 18 tons, were hoisted into position by the two SVR 30 ton steam cranes. A total of 40 tons of steelwork was used in the bridge. It was completed in time for the re-opening of the railway on 5 March 1983. The total cost was £104,981 of which the county council paid £73,487. The £2,995 in the Guarantee Co fund was transferred to the Holdings Co which paid £31,494. So at last the bridge menace which had threatened the railway for fifteen years was firmly disposed of at considerably less cost than had been feared, and the railway looked forward to a secure future. Little did anyone guess how insecure it was!

On 30 April the SVR was justifiably proud in being entrusted with a locomotive from the National Collection, SR 'King Arthur' 4–6–0 No 777 *Sir Lamiel*. This made a return trip from Bridgnorth to Bewdley and back and had just returned to Bewdley when news came through that the embankment just south of the by-pass bridge had collapsed. Bob Massey, driver of 2–10–0 *Gordon* on the 14.10 from Bewdley, on arriving at Bridgnorth reported that he felt the engine wobble as he approached the by-pass bridge. A party set out to inspect and found the embankment tumbling down and rails already suspended in mid air. The cause was fairly obvious. The Highley road below the railway had been lowered to pass under the by-pass. This left the ground below the railway embankment unsupported on the river side and, still fairly sodden after a wet autumn, it had given way. Repairs were put in hand immediately by the County Council on a 'without prejudice' arrangement while responsibility for the damage was settled. It was realised that the collapse was the result of the road works and the railway was relieved of responsibility. The train service north of Hampton Loade was suspended while it was repaired. A good sound job was made of the new embankment and, although now more secure than ever before, it was a cause for concern for a while and was subject to a 5mph speed restriction. On 17 May the BR weed-killing train went up the line as far as the embankment, and the following day trains began running through to Bridgnorth again.

While work on the embankment proceeded, on 7 May another famous member of the National Collection, 2–10–0 No 92220 *Evening Star*, arrived on the SVR. This had the honour of working the first train over the new embankment on 18 May. The 'King Arthur' left on the 13th and so was unable to return to Bridgnorth, but *Evening Star* stayed until the 20th. It was an extraordinary piece of good fortune that neither of these or any other locomotive or a train fell to the bottom of the embankment with injuries and loss of life. The SVR had had its narrowest escape from disaster, emphasising the importance of constant vigilance over the railway formation.

A detail worth mentioning is that on 15 March 1982, exactly ten years after its incorporation, the SVR (Holdings) Co Ltd was re-registered as a public limited company under the Companies Acts 1948-1980. The Guarantee Co was automatically re-designated as a private company. In 1981 the Guarantee Co purchased another 7,000 shares in the Holdings Co, so increasing its holdings to 108,000 shares, 24.72 per cent of the share capital. On 4 June 1982 the authorised share capital of the Holdings Co was increased to £750,000.

Attention was now turning to Kidderminster. Traffic to the sugar factory at Foley Park had ended in 1980, but the line was maintained to connect the SVR to BR. The future of the railway services at Kidderminster, however, looked grim. The train service was so poor, particularly south of

Kidderminster, and loadings so light, that closure between Stourbridge Junction and Worcester was considered. This would have adversely affected the SVR. The situation was saved when, to make way for the High Speed Trains on the Birmingham - Gloucester - Bristol services from 16 May 1983, the locals between Gloucester and Birmingham, formerly via Bromsgrove, were re-routed via Kidderminster. By way of introducing the new services, BR held an exhibition on Saturday 14 May in Kidderminster goods yard, which was closed on that day. To mark the occasion the SVR sent 7812 *Erlestoke Manor* with two coaches to form part of the exhibition. It was followed by 'Kidderminster Rail Week' during which, and for the rest of the month, there were cheap fares to a wide range of places. The new train services consisted of an hourly semi-fast between Birmingham and Worcester stopping only at Cradley Heath, Stourbridge Junction, Kidderminster and Droitwich, and an hourly stopping train between Birmingham and Kidderminster. The publicity paid off and at once passenger loadings began to increase. There are now two expresses an hour between Birmingham and Worcester, most extended to Malvern, Hereford or Cardiff, plus the Kidderminster stopping trains. Many are filled to capacity, pointing to the fact that business is related to quality of service.

With the closure of Kidderminster goods yard, the way was clear for negotiations between the SVR and BR for the extension into Kidderminster. It was agreed that the SVR should pay £75,000 for the section of railway from Foley Park to Kidderminster Junction. It is interesting to compare the prices paid by the SVR for the railway: in 1970 5½ miles from Bridgnorth to Alveley cost £25,000; in 1974 8½ miles from there to beyond Foley Park cost £74,000; in 1984 1 mile to Kidderminster Junction cost £75,000. The remaining quarter mile to Comberton Road, Kidderminster, about 3 acres, was taken on lease from BR at an annual rent of £14,000.

The prospectus inviting shares for the Kidderminster extension was issued on 16 November 1983, and on 15 December the authorised share capital of the company was increased from £750,000 to £1,000,000. The aim of the share issue was to raise a minimum sum of £96,000 to pay for the cost of the railway, the share issue, and professional services, and a maximum of £300,000 to cover the cost of new station buildings and other works in connection with a new terminus. Shareholders' 'dividends' consisted of free tickets: two third class for 25 - 99 shares; four for 100 - 499 shares; four first class for 500 - 999 shares; and a first class family gold pass for 1,000 or more shares.

Like the previous share issue this was an outstanding success and the minimum of £96,000 was cleared by 29 February 1984. While the money was coming in work was going ahead towards a design for the station. After preliminary schemes were rejected the work fell into the hands of Mr R.H. Marrows, an SVR member who was also a qualified architect. Bob Marrows gave his services in the detailed design of a GWR style building based on a design prepared in 1890 by J.E. Danks of the GWR Civil Engineers Department, Paddington, for Ross-on-Wye. Similar buildings were erected at other stations including Stourbridge Town. A double-faced platform (described as an island) was planned to accommodate a ten-coach train on one side and a six-coach train on the other, both with run-round facilities. Because of the downward inclination of the old goods yard towards the south, the formation for the tracks was excavated to provide a level length and the platforms were at ground level which eliminated the necessity for steps up to the station entrance.

By 4 May 1984 the full £300,000 had been subscribed and still the applications were pouring in. This time the management did not make the mistake of returning excess subscriptions, but an extension of the share issue was made. The station platform construction contract was let to Riteway Construction Ltd for £127,000 and in March 1984 excavation began for the tracks on each side of the platform, taking advantage of a temporary tenancy of the Kidderminster site. The contract for the erection of a substantial galvanised steel boundary fence round the entire site was let to Goodman Groggan for

£59,000. The first works train, D1013 *Western Ranger* with the steam crane for track laying, arrived at Kidderminster on 11 May after permission had been granted by BR. By 24 May the platform was completed and the ballast was prepared for the track. Track laying in the platform began early in June and by the time the Light Railway Order was granted, on 21 July, all that remained to be done was the spur from the run-round loop in the bay. The tremendous work carried out by the permanent way gang under Gerry Carter in the limited time available cannot be praised too highly.

The Severn Valley Light Railway Order 1984 came into operation on 21 July. The Schedule defined 'Railway No 1' as extending from the eastern end of the line covered by the LRO of 1973, at Foley Park, to a point 167 metres north east of the bridge under Hoo Road. 'Railway No 2' was to be a new railway 803 metres long at Kidderminster to a point 80 metres south of Comberton Road. Section 8 of the LRO forbade the use of electrical motive power on the railway except from batteries on the locomotive or carriage. Section 9 provided for the limitation of axle weight and speed by the Secretary of State for Transport and forbade the carrying of passengers without his written permission. Contravention renders the company liable to a fine of £50. Section 10 ruled that passengers must be covered by insurance up to one million pounds in case of accident, and adequacy of cover was to be constantly reviewed.

On 23 July the SVR Co paid the £75,000 purchase money to BR. Major Olver inspected the line on 24 July and recommended that opening should be sanctioned. The Severn Valley Light Railway (Transfer) Order was issued shortly afterwards and the first train of passenger coaches, hauled by 6960 *Raveningham Hall* ran through to Kidderminster for clearance tests on the evening of Friday 27 July, arriving at 21.05. While the engine was being reversed over the crossover it was found that the buffer beam cleared the platform by 1/4in, and the platform edge had to be cut back. Last-minute preparations were made on Saturday 28 July, under a grilling sun. In a whirl of intense activity scores of volunteers, including the author and his daughter, prepared the station for business. An old coach was positioned in the bay and was adapted as a booking office. Temporary toilets, bookstall and refreshment hut arose as if out of the ground. The final touches, or blows, were applied on the Sunday, and all was ready.

Monday 30 July 1984 was one of the great days in the history of the SVR. Trains were through to Kidderminster at last. The ceremonial tape was cut by Dr John Prideaux, Director BRB Policy Unit, and the first train, a VIP special, on which the author was privileged to ride, was headed by 4930 *Hagley Hall*, appropriately driven by Gerry Carter, and fired by Roy Baker. The first service train to enter the station was headed by 5690 *Leander*. The junction with BR was passed for passenger traffic on 12 December 1984 and the first through working was on 29 December.

Work on the station building began in autumn 1984, thanks to a grant of £60,000 from the English Tourist Board. The contract for the building was let to William Jackson (Langley Green) Ltd who made an excellent job of the ornate brickwork. The same firm had been involved in reconstructing buildings in the Black Country Museum near Dudley, and had experience in old building techniques. The first stage of the building, the west wing housing the toilets and bookshop, was opened on 24 November 1984. Negotiations for a bank loan, and continuation of the share issue (by 20 January 1985 it had raised £383,000), made it possible to go ahead with the frontage building. This was begun in November 1984 and opened to the public on 28 September 1985. It was officially opened by Michael Spicer MP, Parliamentary Secretary of State for Transport, on 4 July 1986. It comprised a room for use as a tourist information office, the ticket office, booking hall and the 'King and Castle' bar and lounge. The new station is an attractive building, an asset to the SVR and to the town of Kidderminster, and a credit to Bob Marrows.

Meanwhile, on the neighbouring BR station, signs had been erected saying 'Kidderminster / for the Severn Valley Railway'. Six of these were later stupidly replaced by gaudy signs bearing the name 'Midline', the name given to the Birmingham district railway network, as if passengers arriving at a station need to know which line they are on. Outside the station large roadside signs proclaimed both BR and the SVR. The remainder of the goods yard became a joint free car park. The extension into Kidderminster brought an increase in passenger loadings on the SVR. At the end of 1983 the passenger total was 173,968; 1984 181,345 and 1985, the first full year at Kidderminster, 191,619. The extension of the Santa Specials to Kidderminster was almost too successful, causing severe embarrassment at Arley on the second weekend in December. Extra traffic has been generated by the BR/SVR 'Steam Connection' enabling passengers to buy tickets at reduced rates from a wide range of BR stations, including a journey on the SVR from Kidderminster to Bridgnorth and back.

In March 1985 the large goods shed at Kidderminster came onto the market and it was decided that the SVR should purchase it for the carriage and wagon department. Drawings were prepared by Alan Davies at the same time for a new GWR type signal box for Kidderminster, resulting in some curious conflicts with the Wyre Forest planning authorities who pointed out, for example, that the area of glass was excessive and contravened building regulations. After much explanation and discussion planning permission was obtained and the signal box was begun in early March 1986. The finished building, 40ft long, was handed over by the contractor, A.N. Griffiths of Wolverhampton, a week before Christmas. The S&T department was already engaged in its biggest project so far, erecting signals, including a gantry with ten signals, hundreds of yards of signal wire and point rodding and miles of electrical wiring. Four miles of wiring went into the signal box which contains a 62-lever frame, a block shelf 22ft long and a relay room with 70 relays. Much S&T equipment was recovered from Acton in West London, and from Taunton as a result of the West of England re-signalling. The gantry is the first example on a restored railway. For working the section between Bewdley South and Kidderminster it was decided not to use tokens which would cause complications at the passing loop on the approach to Kidderminster station. Instead, an acceptance lever is used in each box in conjunction with track-circuiting. When asked to accept a train the signalman at Bewdley South or Kidderminster reverses his acceptance lever, which he is able to do only if the track circuits are clear. This locks his section signal at danger and also the acceptance lever in the other box. The other signalman can then pull off his section signal which immediately locks the acceptance lever at the opposite end. The signal box was commissioned on the weekend of 21-22 November 1987.

The entire design and installation of the Kidderminster signalling was a magnificent achievement by Alan Davies, John Phillips, David Wittamore and the members of the S&T department. Work inside the signal box consumed 8,000 man-hours, to say nothing of the designing of the signal box itself and the rest of the installation, all carried out voluntarily at no cost to the company. The work of the PW gang in installing the new layout, including the long passing loop which extends nearly to the Hoo Road bridge, was also highly commendable.

At Bridgnorth, local residents complained about boiler rivetting in the open air; also the boiler-smith was suffering the discomfort of working out of doors in all weathers. On 25 March 1986 the outdoor rivetting was banned by a court order. The situation was somewhat absurd in that the housing estate in question was reputed to be built on land originally set aside for industrial development. When the matter was taken to court in Shrewsbury, the judge considered that the case should never have been brought before him and that it should have been dealt with by the Bridgnorth magistrates. Then, when the SVR applied for planning permission for a boiler shop, it was refused but, after a second attempt, was granted late in 1987. Outdoor rivetting was to be banned again from 1 November 1988. The planned building is 100ft x 45ft, equipped with a 30 ton overhead crane, to be completed in 1989 at an estimated cost of £300,000. On 16 May 1988 a new share issue was made whereby it was hoped to raise up to £500,000 by the sale of £1 shares. £150,000 had to be raised by 1 November 1988. By the end of January 1989 it had reached £332,000. The total number of shareholders now exceeds 10,000.

Membership of the Guarantee Co goes on increasing: by August 1986 it had exceeded 13,500. The company continued to purchase shares in the Holdings Co and by 31 December 1986 it held 177,010 shares representing 18.31 per cent of the capital, making it by far the largest shareholder. By the same date the Holdings Co had allotted 966,859 shares, approaching the authorised capital of £1,000,000. With the need for the boiler shop at Bridgnorth and a carriage storage shed at Kidderminster, it was proposed to increase the share capital to £2,000,000. The station facilities at Kidderminster make a substantial contribution; in 1987 £840,000 was generated by sale of tickets (£304,000), the bookshop (£67,500), the 'King and Castle' (£146,000), the refreshment kiosk (£18,700) and various other activities, which easily covers the £14,000 rent to BR. It is hoped eventually to acquire the freehold of the site. In 1983 total turnover was £870,000; in 1987 £1,707,000.

All this can be seen as a measure of the progress made by the SVR in just over twenty years. But it is likely that the next twenty years into the 21st century will prove an even greater test.

CHAPTER 10

Restoring and Stocking the Railway

Before any locomotives or rolling stock could be used on the railway, the track and fixed structures had to be put in order, watering facilities installed or repaired and station platforms cleared of weeds and saplings. At Bridgnorth, where the BR dismantling gang had started to remove track from the station, this had to be relaid. For most members this was their first experience of railway work. The first working party began clearing weeds and rubble at Bridgnorth on 26 September 1965. Considerable foresight was exercised by the Society in the purchase of the ballast inside Bridgnorth tunnel before the bridge over Hollybush Road was demolished at the end of 1966. To gain access to it the siding at Eardington was removed and relaid into the tunnel.

On 25 March 1967 the first locomotive arrived, GWR 0–6–0 No 3205, bringing with it three GWR coaches. From that date a steady stream of locomotives, carriages and wagons came onto the railway. A chronicle of their arrivals would be tedious; the information is contained in the *SVR Stock Book* obtainable at the bookshops at Kidderminster, Bewdley and Bridgnorth stations. It contains illustrations, histories and descriptions, and dimensions of every locomotive and most of the rolling stock and rail mounted equipment such as cranes, trolleys and permanent way machinery, and their dates of arrival on

Notes to this chapter are on p218.

the railway. Updated editions appear from time to time. It is, however, worth mentioning a few items of outstanding interest.

On 10 September 1967 No 3205 was steamed up to haul a works train carrying SVR Society members to clear undergrowth from the Hampton Loade - Alveley section. By the end of 1967 there were four steam locomotives, one railcar (GWR No 22), nine coaches and nine goods vehicles at Bridgnorth. This was a period when BR was withdrawing steam locomotives for cutting up at the rate of hundreds a month. Some were less than ten years old and normally would have had many years of useful life left but, with the prospect of early withdrawal, maintenance was minimal and by the time they were withdrawn many locomotives, though far from old, were in a deplorable state. The same was true of much passenger rolling stock. If interesting historical examples were to be saved, no time could be lost; but it all needed money. Many items were bought privately and moved to the SVR because it was the most convenient site which could provide a home. Several were later removed to other private railways.

While stock was arriving volunteers were restoring the track, structures and signalling equipment. An all-timber signal box, built in 1925 and suitable for Bridgnorth, was found redundant at Pensnett near Brierley Hill. It was carefully dismantled in December 1968 and the top half was re-erected on the slightly shortened brick base at Bridgnorth during the first half of 1969. In the late summer it was handed over by the civil engineering department to the S&T for installation of the frame, interlocking, instruments etc, and for connecting to points and signals. Much of this was removed from Arley with a lack of foresight which gave rise to numerous excuses.

By the end of 1971 the SVR had a stock of seventeen steam locomotives, twenty-three coaches and twenty-six goods wagons. Lack of covered accommodation was beginning to prove a problem. Practically all restoration work on locomotives, carriages and wagons had to be carried out in the open air in all weathers, and afterwards stock had to be stored outdoors where it gradually deteriorated. In late October 1971 BR closed the diesel depot at Heaton Mersey near Stockport and it was brought by the SVR for £100. An SVR team dismantled the shed in April 1972 and it was removed to Bridgnorth over a period of several weeks. The removal was completed in July at a total cost of £187 for dismantling and removal. Another similar shed was removed from Portskewett, between Chepstow and Newport. The sections were later used to erect a shed at Bridgnorth which was brought into use in May 1978 and is now the main workshop, enabling heavy repairs to locomotives to be carried out under cover.

The only steam locomotive to be brought to the SVR in 1972 was LNER K4 class three-cylinder 2–6–0 No 3442 *The Great Marquess* (Darlington 1938), owned by Lord Garnock. It arrived on 9 September and ran for only a short period before being taken out of service for overhaul. It was completely dismantled and was found to need extensive repairs. It proved to be one of the biggest locomotive reconstruction jobs undertaken on the SVR. The tender needed a new tank and bunker; the boiler was in a poor state with cracks in the steel; the chassis needed a complete overhaul; but because of pressure of other work it had to wait its turn in a long queue.

Work began on the tender early in 1984. Wheels and journals were turned during the early summer and axle boxes were repaired. By spring 1985 the Gresley gear and the rest of the motion were completed and by the end of the summer the chassis was ready. Work then began on the boiler and as this progressed the full extent of the work became apparent. The biggest job was the throat plate which had to be removed. A new one was made in Cornwall by Roger Pridham, an outstanding achievement carried out with absolute precision. It was drilled at Bridgnorth and rivetted in place in spring 1987. By this time the new tender tank and bunker had been made and fitted and it was ready for painting by the summer. Work continued on the boiler; the copper tube plate was overhauled and new crown stays were fitted. Late in 1987 the boiler was given a hydraulic test and in January 1988 it was steam-tested up to pressure. All that remained was to fit the new smoke box and mount the boiler on the chassis.

As experience with locomotive work built up there was a steady increase in confidence in the tackling of jobs which earlier would not have been considered. Today the removal of a boiler, fitting new tubes and stays, even making and fitting a new throat plate, or lifting an engine off its wheels and turning up the wheels, is all a matter of routine. Major work is even undertaken for other railways or for the National Railway Museum.

Permanent way maintenance was greatly facilitated by the acquisition, in 1971 and 1972, of two ballast tamping machines from BR at Bilston and Wolverhampton. These have been of great assistance to the PW gang which, despite excellent team work, are only just managing to keep abreast of track deterioration. There are also several petrol trolleys used to convey men quickly to various sites, one of them, an enclosed vehicle, is capable of a high turn of speed. Over the years various other pieces of equipment have been obtained, including off-the-rail vehicles, to assist in handling concrete sleepers which are being installed over ever increasing lengths, and in cutting trenches and drains. For heavy work the railway now has three steam cranes. First to arrive, from Swindon on 31 May 1974, was a 6-ton crane built at Leeds in 1949. A 30-ton breakdown crane by Cowans Sheldon, 1961, with match truck, arrived from Chester on 24 June 1977 and a similar crane was bought from the Keighley & Worth Valley Railway about the same time. In 1985 an old GWR hand crane was bought by the '813 Fund'.

An unfortunate mistake was made in 1974 when a group purchased an 064 class 2–6–2T from German Federal Railways. The price of £2,722 paid on 27 May was certainly not excessive but regrettably the engine's overall width and height were. It was thought at first that it would be able to operate on the railway but, after being steamed once or twice at Bridgnorth, it was sold to the Nene Valley Railway where it is able to operate alongside other continental locomotives without restriction. The money was returned to the shareholders, most of whom re-invested it in other SVR-based groups.

Some of the most interesting restoration work on the SVR has been carried out on GWR 2–8–0 No 2857 (Swindon 1918). The engine was bought at Barry by the '2857 Society' on 20 May 1974 for £5,775 after it had stood there for eleven years. It was brought by rail to Bewdley where it arrived on 13 August 1975. A dedicated team of enthusiasts set to work on it in the spring of 1976 and on 9 September 1979, after replacement of all the small tubes in the boiler, it had its first steam tests. Meanwhile, the tender had been overhauled, with a new coal well, at Wagon Repairs Ltd, Stoke on Trent, and it was returned to Bewdley in January 1978. The repairs, though carried out at low cost, later proved to have been sub-standard. Restoration of the locomotive was completed by early 1980 and during the gala weekend in mid-June it worked a train of goods wagons between Bewdley and Highley. It was then discovered that two superheater flue tubes needed replacing and it was decided to strip the boiler completely for examination. On 24 October 1981 the engine was taken to Bridgnorth where the boiler was removed from the frames, and the chassis was brought back to Bewdley for a thorough overhaul. Earlier a crack had been discovered in one of the cylinder castings. An attempted weld had been unsuccessful, but as the crack did not affect steam passages it was decided to leave it and to try to find a suitable replacement. One was found at Barry on No 2859 but then, by an extraordinary stroke of fortune, a good casting was discovered at the closed Briton Ferry Steelworks in South Wales where it had been hidden under a heap of coal. This was bought and transported to Bewdley. Here it was found that the cylinder and valve bores needed truing up, so the two halves were taken apart and machined up at Hugh Phillips Engineering Ltd at Tredegar. The biggest job was removing the old cylinder block. The twenty-two fitted bolts securing it to the frames took eleven weekends to remove, all this outdoors in all weathers. The new cylinder block fitted perfectly. New valve liners were cast from fresh patterns and on 9 July 1983 they were contracted in liquid nitrogen and inserted. New pistons had to be made, and everything accurately lined up. On the frames it took seven months to grind the axlebox horns to the required standard of accuracy, and on 10 November 1984 the engine was re-wheeled. On 27 March 1985 the newly overhauled boiler was replaced and, after fitting of remaining parts, the engine was steamed on 18 August. Only three weeks later the 2–8–0 was off to South Wales with a train of SVR freight wagons to take part in the 'Freight Spectacular' at Newport in connection with the GW 150 celebrations. This was a high honour indeed. Since its return it has proved an excellent runner on passenger trains between Kidderminster and Bridgnorth. On 27 June 1987 it made light work of a 14-coach special from Bridgnorth to Bewdley.

A basic need on the SVR has always been a turntable. Turning locomotives and other items of rolling stock periodically will help to equalise flange wear which, without a turntable, is uneven. It will also allow visiting locomotives to be turned and will assist with filming contracts. One at each end of the line would be ideal, but there is nowhere to put one at Bridgnorth. Space is available at Bewdley in the angle between the Kidderminster and Stourport lines, and at Kidderminster one is included in the planned layout. In July - September 1974 the turntable at Whitchurch on the Shrewsbury - Crewe line was bought and removed to Bewdley where it has been stored ever since. A second turntable was bought from the Bluebell Railway in Sussex in June 1981. It was moved to Bewdley on the 19th and was stored on the course of the former Tenbury line north of Bewdley station.

In 1977 the SVR was honoured by being entrusted with LMS class 5 4–6–0 No 5000 (Crewe 1935) from the National Collection, belonging to the National Railway Museum at York. It arrived on 19 November 1977 and was given a complete overhaul at Bridgnorth, entering traffic in June 1979. Besides working regular SVR trains it has frequently been out on the main line.

Opposition was experienced in September 1978 towards

the bringing to the SVR of two 'Western' diesel-hydraulic locomotives, D1013 (Swindon 1962) and D1062 (Crewe 1963). It was thought by some members that this was betraying the original intention of the SVR Society to preserve the line as a steam railway. The Westerns have proved popular in conjunction with other diesels at 'diesel weekends', drawing to the railway a completely different type of enthusiast. In occasional emergencies they have been used to replace steam locomotives which have broken down; that is, of course, if the Westerns are not also out of use for the same reason.

The most extraordinary locomotive to appear on the SVR was the LNWR 2–2–2 No 3020 *Cornwall*, on loan for five years from the National Collection, originally built at Crewe in 1847 and much rebuilt. It was towed to Bewdley by a Class 47 and arrived on 16 August 1979. It was taken on to Bridgnorth where the intention was to restore it to working order and to use it for a period of five years. However, when work on it was about to begin, the boiler inspector's hammer went straight through the bottom of the boiler. It was realised that the cost of a full repair was more than could be afforded and so the engine was removed by road to York on 6 September 1982. At the same time the Department of Education & Science bought the SNCF 4–6–0 from the Nene Valley Railway, where it remains.

In 1979 the SVR won an award from the Association of Railway Preservation Societies for the greatest number of steam locomotives restored for service in one year. These were the 2-8–0 2857, 'Manor' 4–6–0 No 7812, 2–6–2T No 5164, 'Hall' class 4–6–0 No 4930 (all ex Barry) and Class 5 4–6–0 No 5000.

In the decade from the opening of the SVR in May 1970 to May 1980 the locomotive with the highest mileage was 2–6–0 No 46443 which ran 29,010 miles. Next was Class 5 4–6–0 45110 with 21,185 miles. The latter worked during every year and the 2–6–0 in all but 1980. From 1975 2–6–2T No 4566 achieved the third highest mileage of 18,420. Class 4 2–6–0 43106 came fourth with 17,617 in spite of not running during four years. The highest mileage in one year was achieved by 7819 *Hinton Manor* in 1979 with 5,760 miles, followed by 2–6–0 46443 in the same year with 5,360 miles[1]. These mileages may seem low to the average motorist, but they represent running on possibly about a hundred days in the year.

At the end of 1979 there were thirty-four locomotives, fifty-five passenger coaches and fifty-four assorted goods vehicles on the railway together with various vans, trolleys and cranes used in maintenance work. Apart from those under repair in the workshop at Bridgnorth or in the paintshop at Bewdley, all these had to be stored out of doors. Proposals were made for a three-road carriage shed in the cutting on the 'Stourport siding' but after high quotations in 1979 the matter was deferred. It is now intended to erect the shed in Kidderminster.

For many years, at the south end of the Bewdley island platform, there stood a cast-iron urinal of a sort once common on our stations and streets. It was probably installed after February 1896 when the GWR Traffic Committee approved the erection of a urinal and other additional works at Bewdley station at a total cost of £100. At some time before the SVR took over a PW inspector, possibly with an excess of hygienic scruples, ordered its demolition, but it was thought by various SVR members that its restoration would be an asset. The problem was where to find another. At last, in 1976, one was discovered at the abandoned Melrose station on the former NBR Waverley Route.[2] It was bought, dismantled with considerable difficulty on a freezing day in January 1977, brought to Bewdley and re-erected. Its day of glory came on 10 September when it was decorated with flags and officially opened by the mayor of Bewdley. It was certainly a unique occasion in his term of office, and one of those light-hearted episodes which probably help to maintain a degree of sanity on the railway.[3]

A particularly noteworthy piece of carriage restoration was carried out on GWR Churchward saloon No 9055 (Swindon 1912) bought in 1972 and rebuilt as an invalid saloon for wheelchair passengers. It was completed early in 1986.

The Ruston 165hp 0–4–0 diesel shunter obtained in 1972 had proved its value so in 1980, when four more became available on the closure of the Patent Shaft Steelworks at Wednesbury, it was decided to purchase them and they were delivered on 22 October. They were all built by Ruston in 1957; three were diesel-mechanical, of which two were used for spares, and one was diesel-electric. For moving stock around at Bewdley and Bridgnorth, where the Rustons were under-powered, two BR class 08 diesel-electric 0–6–0 shunters were obtained. A more powerful locomotive was also needed in the PW department where heavy trains of material and equipment needed to be moved at higher speed. In 1987 a BR class 25 Bo-Bo diesel-electric No 25904 was purchased; it arrived early in 1988.

From time to time locomotives from other railway preservation societies or from the National Collection visit the SVR for a period. Examples have been 2–10–0 No 92220 *Evening Star* and SR 'King Arthur' 4–6–0 No 777 *Sir Lamiel*, both from the National Collection, in April and May 1983; GWR 4–4–0 *City of Truro,* also from the National Collection, which was overhauled at Bridgnorth and completed in August 1985; LNWR Webb 0–6–2 'Coal Tank' No 1054 from Dinting Railway Centre in September and October 1986; and Somerset & Dorset Joint Railway 2–8–0 No 53809 from the Midland Railway Centre, Butterley in October 1987. Other visitors have been 'Castle' class 4–6–0 No 7029 *Clun Castle* from Birmingham Railway Museum; and No 5051 *Drysllwyn Castle* and 'Hall' class No 6998 *Burton Agnes Hall* from Didcot Railway Centre. SVR locomotives have operated special trains on BR main lines. While these movements are expensive, they attract considerable notice to the SVR and so contribute towards its financial stability.

In common with other privately preserved railways, and with BR in particular, vandalism has been a severe problem on the SVR. The worst area is around Kidderminster which, for a town of its size, has an alarmingly high crime rate, and there have been many attacks on trains between Bewdley tunnel and Foley Park which have caused the company much extra work and great expense in the replacement of broken windows. No part of the railway can be considered immune from this disease of modern society. This is the more regrettable in view of the superb standard of work carried out by the carriage & wagon department at both Bewdley and Bridgnorth. A small team of paid staff and volunteers produce a standard of finish which could not be exceeded anywhere, but it is sad to see it deteriorate so rapidly, or suffer deliberate damage, because of lack of covered accommodation.

One of the most important aspects of running the railway is the training of firemen, drivers, guards and signalmen, all of whom require considerable knowledge, and ability to pass examinations at the end of a course of training. Unlike a railway run by full-time employees, because many volunteers can manage to work on the railway for only a limited number of days in a year, a great many more are required. For instance, to operate the seven signal boxes at Kidderminster, Bewdley South and North, Arley, Highley, Hampton Loade and Bridgnorth, it is necessary to have a pool of about a hundred qualified signalmen to draw upon. With a full-time staff a dozen or less would suffice. To operate the trains there are about sixty to seventy drivers and a roughly equal number of firemen and guards. As can be imagined, the roster clerks have a busy time keeping the duties covered and coping with sudden cancellations. They can run up a heavy telephone bill. To run a train from Bridgnorth to Kidderminster requires not only a driver, fireman, guard, and two travelling ticket inspectors, but a lighter-up, cleaner, someone to coal the tender, carriage cleaners and someone to fill the carriage water tanks, at least six signalmen, six stationmasters or other senior staff, booking clerks and other assistant station staff, and three PW lengthmen.

A volunteer who turns up at the SVR with the idea of becoming an engine driver in a few weeks is doomed to disappointment. He may have to start his training by shovelling ashes out of a pit in several inches of half-frozen water, spending many tedious hours cleaning locomotives, coaling tenders and carrying out other menial tasks, for two or three years before he can be accepted for training as a fireman. Having qualified in this capacity he has still a long course of training before he can pass as a driver. Signalmen, as with drivers and guards, have to pass examinations on rules and regulations and then have to be passed out on the individual signal boxes. Constant checks are necessary to ensure that high standards are maintained, and after a long absence a volunteer will be required to take a refresher course and to be re-examined.

The greatest financial burden to be borne is maintenance of fixed assets and rolling stock, not merely to contain deterioration, but constantly to improve standards. Hundreds of thousands of pounds could immediately be swallowed up in urgently needed repairs to Bewdley viaduct which, when carried out, will contribute nothing to the attraction of visitors who will be unaware of the work. As mentioned in chapters 4 and 6, the unstable ground through which the line passes has been a menace since 1861, and will remain so. Constant vigilance is necessary at cuttings and embankments, the five viaducts and Bewdley tunnel. Culverts also need watching: if one is blocked water will rapidly build up and will undermine or even wash away an embankment.

A matter which cannot be overlooked is that the railway offers to the public only a form of entertainment: it does not carry essential goods, mail or minerals, neither does it carry passengers on vital journeys connected with their work or travels. It is thus at the mercy of whims and fancies. Another danger is that we now have a generation of adults who never knew steam traction at large on BR and who were not fired with the keen enthusiasm as were many born earlier. There is, of course, the novelty of a ride in a train. Since the spread of private motoring from the 1950s many reach adulthood having never travelled in a train. For them it makes little difference if their SVR train is hauled by *Leander* or *Western Ranger*. The railway can no longer rely entirely on the attraction of steam power. Courtesy, unobtrusive efficiency, punctuality, and tidy stations become increasingly important. Certainly the SVR makes great efforts in this direction, but the efforts can never be relaxed, and this places constant demands on the paid staff and volunteers engaged in operation. The SVR, like other private railways, has its hard core of 'dyed-in-the-wool' steam enthusiasts who, despite their valuable contribution, maintain a 'blinkered' outlook on other forms of motive power. Fortunately it is an attitude limited to a fairly small number and is unlikely to increase. As boiler shells, fireboxes and cylinders wear out the ever present financial problems of maintaining steam operation will become greater, and more reliance may have to be placed on the diesels. On the other hand, the diesel enthusiasts can be equally blinkered.

A valuable source of income is provided by filming for television and the cinema. The SVR has frequently been called upon to provide station or train scenes, some representing Victorian or Edwardian periods. The filming is made mid-week, mostly during slack times in spring or early summer, but sometimes in the autumn or winter. Station yards become crammed with vans, cables trail around everywhere, and brilliant lights illuminate a scene of apparent confusion as a train moves to and fro.

An aspect of the organisation which troubles some members is the pressure towards commercialisation, despite the need for the railway to make every pound it can, and a tendency to lose sight of the historical importance of the preservation movement. The 'working museum' function of the old engines and rolling stock as well as the stations and signal boxes, must not be overlooked. This does attract passengers. Market research can establish how many passengers are travelling on the railway for the second, third or fourth time. It is these passengers who are the most important for the future of the railway, and their numbers will vary inversely with the cost of the fare. The supply of first-time travellers is bound to run out. The author has, on more than one occasion, told a man the fare and heard him say to his wife and children, 'Well, all right; just this once.' His decision may depend on nothing more than the distance he has come in the car. Half fares for members and reductions for senior citizens attract passengers who may not have come if required to pay the full fare, and they also attract people into membership. Pricing policy is certainly a tight-rope exercise, but over-commercialisation, high fares and unrepresentative rolling stock could destroy the original object of the organisation which was to preserve an historic branch line and to show people what the country railway was like before the second world war. Long may it continue to do this, even with post-war examples of motive power, and so to justify the faith and industry of the founder members.

One final point: in the course of time there is only the past and the future. Everything that happens immediately passes into history and can never be eradicated. Politicians may never learn from history, but railway operators must. This book has shown that the history of the SVR is sufficiently varied for a wealth of knowledge, experience and, dare we hope, wisdom, to be drawn from it to carry the railway forward into a secure future.

Notes

Notes to Chapter 1

1 Forrest, H.E., 'Glacial Lake Severn', *Transactions of the Caradoc and Severn Valley Field Club* 1939.
2 Ekwall, Eilert, *English River Names* Oxford University Press 1968
3 Randall, J., *The Tourist's Guide to Bridgnorth* 1875.
4 *A description and history of Ironbridge Gorge*, Ironbridge Gorge Museum Trust (nd).
5 Plan and profile of proposed railway Bewdley to Kidderminster, September 1801, Birmingham (Local History) Library 527508A.
6 Mutton, Norman, 'The Forges at Eardington and Hampton Loade' from *Transactions of the Shropshire Archaeological Society* Vol LVIII 1967-8 pub 1970. 'Eardington Forges and Canal Tunnel', *Industrial Archaeology* Vol 7 No 1 February 1970. Hadfield, Charles, *The Canals of the West Midlands* 1966.
7 Edward Leader Williams was the father of Sir Edward Leader Williams (1828-1910), engineer of the Manchester Ship Canal, and of Benjamin Williams Leader (1831-1923) the Worcestershire landscape artist.

Notes to Chapter 2

1 Minutes of SVR Board. Public Record Office, Kew (PRO) Ref RAIL 606/1.
2 *Worcestershire Chronicle and Provincial Railway Gazette* 6

October 1852. p8. Reprinted in *Herapath's Railway Journal* 9 October 1852 p 1116.
3 *House of Commons Journal* 1853 p 615
4 The name of Ironbridge is frequently spelt as two words. As will be seen later, the station name was changed from one to two words. Although the Ordnance Survey continues to print Iron Bridge, the town and Museum Trust use the single word form.
5 *Herapath* 11 June 1853 p 629; 18 June p 648; 2 July p 702.
6 House of Lords Record Office, Evidence, HL 1853, Severn Valley Railway.

Notes to Chapter 3

1 *Herapath* 24 September 1853 p 1045.
2 *Minutes of Proceedings*, Institution of Civil Engineers Vol 15 1855-6 pp93-4.
3 *Herapath* 16 June 1855 pp 596-7; Minutes of Shareholders' meetings PRO Kew RAIL 606/4 (Micro-film copy in Shrewsbury Library).
4 House of Lords Record Office. Evidence HL 1855 Severn Valley Railway.
5 Randall, J. *Tourists' Guide to Bridgnorth* 1875. Rep Shropshire Libraries 1982 pp 62-6.
6 *Herapath* 19 April 1856 pp 428, 439.
7 *Herapath* 12 July 1856 p 717.
8 PRO RAIL 606/8.

Notes to Chapter 4

1 Min Proc ICE Vol 58 1878-9 p 339.
2 *Eddowes's Shrewsbury Journal* 25 August and 8 September 1858.
3 *Herapath* 26 February 1859 p 235.
4 *The Worcestershire Chronicle* 30 November 1859 p 2.
5 *Herapath* 13 August 1859 p 829.

6 *Berrows Worcester Journal* 17 December 1859.
7 *Herapath* 4 August 1860 p 760.
8 *Herapath* 12 January 1861 p 46.
9 *The Engineer* 21 June 1861 p 373.
10 Trinder, Barrie (Ed), *Victorian Shrewsbury* Studies in the history of a County Town. Shropshire Libraries, 1984.
11 *Berrows Worcester Journal* 22 June 1861.
12 *Berrows Worcester Journal* 18 May 1861.
13 Eddowes's Shrewsbury Journal 29 January 1862 p 5.
14 PRO MT29/22.
15 PRO MT29/23.
16 *Eddowes's Shrewsbury Journal* 22 January 1862.
17 *Eddowes's Shrewsbury Journal* 5 February 1862; *Birmingham Daily Post* and *Birmingham Journal* 1 February 1862; *The Worcestershire Chronicle* 5 February 1862.
18 PRO RAIL 606/9.

Notes to Chapter 5

1 Under the GWR (West Midland Amalgamation) Act 13 July 1863 c108 Section 5.
2 Much Wenlock & Severn Junction Railway Act 21 July 1859 c26.
3 Under the Great Western, Birmingham & Chester Railways Consolidation Act 7 August 1854 c222 Section 1.
4 Wellington & Severn Junction Railway Act 20 August 1853 c214.
5 Under Section 20 of the GWR (Lightmoor & Coalbrookdale) Act 1 August 1861 c204.
6 By the GWR Act 28 June 1892 c133.
7 *Eddowes's Shrewsbury Journal* 16 November 1864.
8 GWR (Lightmoor to Coalbrookdale) Act 1 August 1861 c204.
9 *Eddowes's Shrewsbury Journal* 28 December 1864.
10 Authorised by Section 37 of the GWR (Additional Powers) Act 5 July 1865 c299.

11 Under sections 37 and 40 of the GWR Act of 7 August 1896 c232.
12 *Herapath* 12 October 1861 p 1043.
13 *Herapath* 13 December 1862 p 1295.
14 *Eddowes's Shrewsbury Journal* 10 August 1864.
15 Shrewsbury & Hereford (Leasing) Act 29 July 1862 c198 Section 3.
16 Under the GWR (Further Powers) Act 30 July 1866 c307 Section 75.
17 Minutes of the GWR Board, PRO RAIL 250/20.
18 *Kidderminster Shuttle* 14 June 1873.
19 *Railway Times* 14 June 1873 p 606.
20 Gooch, Daniel, *Memoirs and Diary* David & Charles 1972.
21 *Railway Times* 30 August 1873 pp 874-5.
22 A full report of the evidence of the Select Committee of the House of Commons on the WSR Bill appears in the *Kidderminster Shuttle* 20 March 1875.
23 GWR Act 19 July 1875 (ch 124) Section 37.
24 *Railway Times* 26 February 1876 p 209.
25 *Kidderminster Shuttle* 12 and 19 January 1878.
26 PRO MT29/39; *Kidderminster Shuttle* 23 March 1878; *Kidderminster Times* 30 March 1878.
27 *Kidderminster Times* and *Kidderminster Shuttle*, 25 May and 1 June 1878.

Notes to Chapter 6

1 PRO MT6 24/49 and MT29/22.
2 Shropshire, Worcestershire & Staffordshire Electric Power Act 8 August 1918 c43.
3 Shropshire, Worcestershire & Staffordshire Electric Power (Consolidation) Act 13 July 1938 c58.
4 Barfield, A.T. in *Railway World* July 1973 pp 302-3.
5 Alfred Baldwin was appointed to the GWR Board in 1903 and became its chairman in 1905. He was MP for Bewdley. His son Stanley, born at Bewdley in 1867, became prime minister.

6 Minutes of Committee, Staffs & Worcs Canal Co, PRO RAIL 871.
7 PRO RAIL 252/48.
8 *The Railway World* Vol VII 2 June 1898.
9 GWR Act 31 July 1914 c107.
10 Clinker, C.R., *Railway World* August 1955 p 185.
11 *GWR Magazine* December 1910 pp 313-14.
12 Min Proc ICE Vol 190 1911-12 Part 4 pp 43-4.
13 *SVR News* No 58 Winter 1980-1.
14 Full information on Arley station can be found in *The SVR at Arley* by Barrie Geens. Wild Swan Publications 1985.
15 An article on the Billingsley and Kinlet railways, by John Tennent, was published in *SVR News* No 24, Summer 1972.
16 PRO MT29/56.

Notes to Chapter 7

1 Shropshire County Record Office (SCRO) DP 389.
2 Worcestershire County Record Office f161/204.
3 SCRO DP 411.
4 SCRO DP 427; DP 444.
5 SCRO DP 448
6 SCRO DP 454.
7 SCRO DP 472.
8 SCRO DP 497.
9 SCRO DP 706.
10 Beddoes, Keith, 'The Wolverhampton and Bridgnorth Road Motor Services' *SVR News* No 82 Winter 1986-7.
11 For a full history see Williams, Ned, *The Railway to Wombourn*, Uralia Press, 1986, ISBN 0 951 1223 2 0.

Notes to Chapter 8

1 MacDermot, E.T., *History of the GWR* Vol 1 p 611.
2 A copy of the plan is held in the PRO, (RAIL 245/35), and another is in the Shrewsbury Local History Library (R29).
3 PRO MT 29/44.

4 PRO MT 29/47.
5 PRO MT 29/56.
6 PRO MT 29/58.
7 PRO MT 29/75.
8 *Locos of the GWR* Part 3, Railway Correspondence & Travel Society 1956 pp 32-3.
9 Beddoes, Keith, 'Kidderminster Motive Power Depot', *SVR News* No 16 Spring 1970.
10 *Berrow's Worcester Journal* 31 December 1904.
11 *Locos of the GWR* Parts 11 and 13, RCTS 1956 and 1983.
12 Price, M.R.C., *The Cleobury Mortimer & Ditton Priors Light Railway* Oakwood Press 1963; Smith, W., and Beddoes, K., *The Cleobury Mortimer & Ditton Priors Light Railway*, Oxford Publishing Co 1980, SBN 86093 053X; *The Locomotive Magazine* June 1921.
13 *Bridgnorth Journal* 21 January 1928; *SVR News* No 2 February 1966.

Notes to Chapter 9

1 *Kidderminster Shuttle* Friday 2 July 1965.
2 *SVR News* No 13 July 1969 p 3 Article by R.H. Dunn.
3 *The Times* 29 June 1973.

Notes to Chapter 10

1 *SVR News* No 58 Winter 1980-1 p 34.
2 A photograph of it appears on p 235 of *The Railway Station - a Social History* by Jeffrey Richards and John MacKenzie, Oxford University Press 1986.
3 *SVR News* No 45 Autumn 1977 p 26.

Acknowledgements

I am most grateful to the following for supplying information, photographs and other assistance, and for their interest in the project: Keith Beddoes and Columb Howell for information concerning the rescue and preservation of the SVR; Timothy Guest and Peter Jordan for help with the signalling history; Harry Horton of Manchester Library for many details from Bradshaw timetables; and Peter Baughan for supplying photographs taken on a journey shortly before the line closed. My sons Simon and Andrew both read through the draft manuscript and suggested numerous improvements. David Postle supplied other information. I am also grateful to the staffs of the public libraries at Birmingham, Kidderminster, Shrewsbury and Worcester, the House of Lords Record Office, the Public Record office at Kew, and the County Record Offices at Shrewsbury, Stafford and Worcester. The photograph of the SVR timetable of 1862 is reproduced by permission of the Libarian, Kidderminster.

J M
Bewdley

Index

Page numbers in **bold** indicate illustrations